The

WEATHER BOOK

MICHAEL OARD

Master
Books

First printing, March 1997
Second printing, November 1997

For information write: Master Books,
P. O. Box 727, Green Forest, AR 72638

ISBN: 0-89051-211-6

Dedication

This book is dedicated to my oldest son, David, his wife, Tasha, and their family.

Acknowledgments

I especially want to thank my wife for her assistance throughout the preparation of the manuscript and for rewriting several sections, plus several of the creative ideas within the text. I appreciate all the many hours that Gloria Clanin has labored in the preparation of this book, especially for some of her ideas that were added to the manuscript and for her desire to learn more about the weather. I would like to thank Ron Hight for the illustrations that help make the book a valuable learning tool. Thanks also to Jim Young for the final editing of the manuscript.

Table of Contents

Introduction

There are days when the sun shines from a cloudless sky and warm breezes cause the leaves to flutter. Other days are gray, cloudy, and drizzly. What we decide to do for the day often depends upon the weather. If it is a cold and dreary Saturday, we play inside. A heavy snow inspires us to build a snow fort. The weather also determines how we dress for the day.

Weather even affects our moods. A breeze gently kisses your cheek, giving you a sense of peace. It whistles around the corners of your home, howls down your chimney, and might make you feel anxious. Have you noticed the bright smiles a sunny day brings, especially after bad weather?

The weather not only changes our plans for play, but it also affects many other decisions. Businessmen listen to the weather report so they can plan their work more effectively. If your father is a cement contractor, he needs to know if it is too cold, or too wet, to pour his cement. He has to know the regional climate to decide which mix of cement will last the longest. Airports need to know weather conditions so they can advise pilots.

The Bible tells us in John 1:10 that Jesus created everything: "The world was made through Him." The apostle Paul says in the first chapter of the Book of Colossians that He created the atmosphere and the weather: "For by him all things were created: things in heaven and on earth, visible and invisible."

By observing nature's order and beauty, we learn much about Jesus, the Creator of the universe. What does the beauty of sunrises and sunsets teach us about Him? What do we learn when we view awesome mountain ranges? When we look at the fertile valleys and plains with grain ready for harvest, do we see God as our provider? Does the waterfall crashing against the rocks remind us of His strength?

When we know more about God's order, we can predict the number of hours of daylight, the seasons, and the weather. His order is seen as the sun rises and sets, marking each day. Seasons have come and gone since at least the time of the great flood of Noah's day. Life-sustaining rain and snow regularly water the world around us. Weather is part of the system God uses to preserve and nourish His plants and animals. In this way He makes the planet livable for humans. It is only because our God gave us an ordered planet that we can predict the weather. As we grow in our understanding of the physical laws God uses to sustain order in the universe and on earth, we can become better weatherpersons.

Sometimes the harmony we have come to expect in nature appears out of whack. A terrible storm destroys homes and crops. Hail pelts a field

best friends with God, Adam and Eve needed to be free. You wouldn't want a best friend who was forced to love you. It's difficult to have a loving relationship with someone who has no choice. God gave Adam and Eve the freedom to choose, but they wanted it all. They thought they would be like God. They chose to know both good and evil. They couldn't have it both ways because God is all good. They had to leave paradise.

The world they entered as a result of their choices was very different. They came to know evil. Animals ate each other, people died, and sometimes the weather went crazy. As the Bible says, death entered the world. Now we have good and evil living side by side.

We cannot judge Adam and Eve too harshly. We probably would have done the same thing. We're all curious and often want to know more about both good and evil. Sometimes we forget that evil can take us far from God. In our world we have many more choices than Adam and Eve. Every day we decide whether to love God or disobey His commands.

God's laws are all good. If we choose to love and obey His commands, we will experience the harmony, love, and joy a good relationship with Him brings. We will also enjoy good relationships with other people. This is what God desires for us.

So we see that the world changed because of Adam and Eve's choices. As a result, we sometimes experience dangerous storms and other difficulties. But God showed us His mercy by offering us forgiveness through a Saviour, Jesus. He also gave us minds so we can learn about the laws governing the weather and to predict storms.

of grain and destroys a farmer's crops and income within minutes. A sudden tornado crushes a mobile home. A winter blizzard ties up traffic and breaks electrical lines, causing power outages.

Have you ever wondered why God, who is so good, allows His creation to be interrupted by short periods of dangerous weather? We find the answer in the Old Testament Book of Genesis. There is another principle at work in our world. It is called the sin principle. God, in the beginning, declared His creation "very good." It was perfect. There was no death or sickness. The lion and the lamb were friends. Instead of the lion eating the lamb, he ate plants. Best of all, the weather was lovely everywhere. There was perfect order and harmony.

Chapter 3 of the Book of Genesis then tells how this all changed. Adam and Eve were given a choice. With a little help from Satan, they disobeyed God's only command — to not eat the fruit from "the tree of the knowledge of good and evil" (Gen. 2:17). You may wonder why God gave them any command at all. For them to be

Chapter 1
God Created

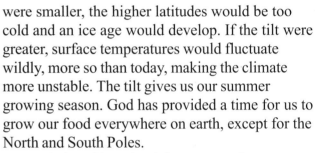

God used His infinite wisdom to create this earth. From the smallest to the largest feature of creation, He displays His intelligence, love, and careful attention to detail.

God placed the moon 240,000 miles (384,000 km) away from the earth — exactly the right distance to cause small tides in the ocean. If the moon were a little closer, it would cause severe tides and flooding. If it were only 50,000 miles (80,000 km) away instead of 240,000 miles, the tides would cover most of the continents twice a day. If the moon were farther away, much of the ocean would become heavily polluted. Tides mix the ocean water. The mixing helps to keep the oceans fresh by exposing more of the water to sunlight and by dispersing pollution. The amount of water in the ocean is important as well, because the oceans are large enough to dilute pollution.

Did you know that the sun is 400 times the size of the moon, and its distance is 400 times the distance of the moon from the earth? That is why the sun and moon, the greater and lesser lights of Genesis 1:16, look the same size in the sky.

The earth spins on its axis at just the right speed — once around every day. If it spun slower, the light side would be too hot for life and the dark side would be too cold. If the earth spun any faster it would cause fierce winds to blow.

If the earth's tilt were smaller, the higher latitudes would be too cold and an ice age would develop. If the tilt were greater, surface temperatures would fluctuate wildly, more so than today, making the climate more unstable. The tilt gives us our summer growing season. God has provided a time for us to grow our food everywhere on earth, except for the North and South Poles.

God placed just the right amount of water vapor and carbon dioxide in the atmosphere. Our ocean is the right size to maintain the proper balance of water vapor in the atmosphere. These gases cause the earth to act like a giant greenhouse. If there were much less of these gases, the earth would be too cold. Although these invisible gases make up about 0.1 percent of the atmosphere, they cause the earth to be about 60°F (35°C) warmer. If there were much more of these gases, the earth would be too hot.

God put exactly the right amount of oxygen in the atmosphere. The atmosphere is composed of about 21 percent oxygen, 78 percent nitrogen, 0.9 percent

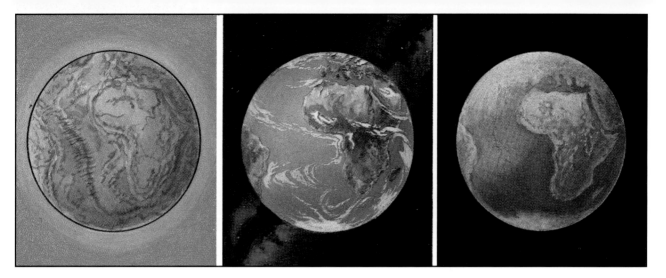

God placed the earth exactly the right distance from the sun — 93 million miles. If it were just a little closer to the sun, it would be too hot for life to exist. If the earth were farther away, it would be too cold and all water on earth would be frozen.

argon, and about 0.15 percent water vapor and carbon dioxide. If there were more oxygen, the processes in our bodies would react too fast. More oxygen would cause fires to burn so quickly that they would provide less sustained warmth and more danger. Forest fires would rage completely out of control. If there were less oxygen in our atmosphere, processes in our bodies would operate too slowly.

The oxygen level also is responsible for the amount of ozone in the stratosphere. Ozone protects us from most of the dangerous ultraviolet rays that come from the sun by absorbing them. This type of light causes skin cancer in man and animals. A little ultraviolet light still gets through, so we use sunscreen to protect our skin.

The atmosphere's thickness protects us from the 20 million meteors that hit the earth each day at speeds averaging 10 miles/sec. The vast majority burn up before they reach the ground.

God even made the earth just the right size for gravity to hold earth's water and the atmosphere in place.

Our world was specially created with design and purpose. In many other ways, Jesus made sure that this world would be a good home for us. For those who choose to listen, all creation shouts of His wondrous works and His love:

> *For the invisible things of him from the creation of the world are clearly seen, being understood by the things that are made, even his eternal power and Godhead; so that they are without excuse (Romans 1:20).*

Chapter 2
What Causes Weather

Weather is the momentary condition of the air. Besides temperature and precipitation, it includes wind direction and wind speed, visibility, the amount of water vapor, air pressure, cloud conditions, and air quality. Precipitation is moisture that falls from the sky in the form of rain, freezing rain, snow, hail, or drizzle. Air quality is determined by how much dust, haze, or pollution is in the air.

The weather also depends on the latitude and how close to the ocean you are. During winter in the Northern Hemisphere, it is usually very cold in Saskatchewan, Canada, while in Texas the weather is mild. Summer temperatures are cooler in northern Europe than in southern Europe. It makes a difference whether you live in Seattle, Washington, close to the ocean, or in Bismarck, North Dakota, far from the ocean at the same latitude.

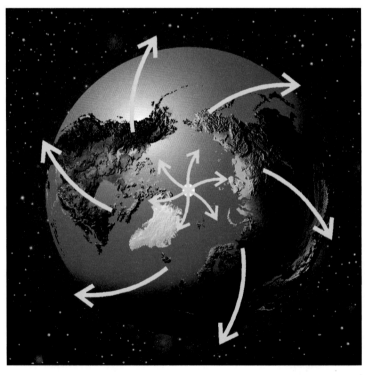

Coriolis Force
As the earth spins toward the east, the air flow in the Northern Hemisphere tends to veer to the right and in the Southern Hemisphere to the left.

The Weather Engine

The sun is the ultimate cause of weather. As sunlight enters the atmosphere its rays are either absorbed by the air or reflected back to space from the white clouds. Sunlight that makes it to the ground is both absorbed and reflected. Most of the reflected light goes back into space. The sunlight absorbed at the earth's surface heats the ground. As the surface warms, it heats the atmosphere above it.

The ground and atmosphere continually lose heat by *infrared radiation* (invisible rays that cool the land at night). Many of these infrared rays are absorbed by the atmosphere, but those that escape into space cause the cooling. Clouds act like a blanket to keep the earth warmer at night. They absorb most of the infrared radiation and redirect some of it back to the ground. As a result, the ground and air below the clouds do not cool off much at night.

The infrared radiation cools the earth at night. When the sun comes up, the sunshine warms the ground and air. This is why the air cools at night and warms during the day. If the days are long and the nights short during summer, more heat is gained by sunshine than is lost by infrared radiation in a 24-hour period. So temperatures warm as summer approaches. It works the opposite in winter. The shorter days and longer nights result in more loss of heat in a 24-hour period. As winter comes, temperatures become colder.

The difference between daytime sunshine and night-time infrared cooling also causes temperature differences between the tropics and polar latitudes. These temperature differences cause an air pressure change, which pushes the earth's winds. Air blows from high pressure to low pressure. For example, the air inside a tire is at a higher pressure than the atmosphere. There are more air molecules per cubic inch or cubic centimeter in the tire than in the atmosphere. So when you loosen the valve, the air flows out of the tire. It works the same way in the atmosphere.

Because of the earth spinning on its axis, air flow in the atmosphere is more complicated. The spin causes air to move to the right in the Northern Hemisphere and to the left in the Southern Hemisphere. This deflecting force on air is called the Coriolis force. As air blows from high to low pressure, the Coriolis force causes it to circulate in a spiral around the low pressure center. The air spirals counterclockwise around a low center in the Northern Hemisphere and clockwise in the Southern Hemisphere. Because the air is spiraling towards the center of the low, it is forced upward, forming clouds and precipitation.

The Coriolis force in the Northern Hemisphere is like a disk rotating counterclockwise. Pretend you are at the center of the disk. If you throw a ball toward a target on the edge of the disk, the ball will miss to the right. It will appear that the ball was deflected to the right. What really happened was that as the ball reached the edge, the disk rotated to the left underneath the ball. It works the same in the atmosphere as the earth rotates.

Air generally rises at the equator. From there it spreads north and south. Air sinks at about 30° latitude. At that latitude it hits the ground and is forced both north and south. The air spreading back toward the equator forms a closed circulation. Two other closed circulations are found in the middle and high latitudes of each hemisphere. The earth has a total of six circulations. This is the planet's average or general circulation caused by the weather engine.

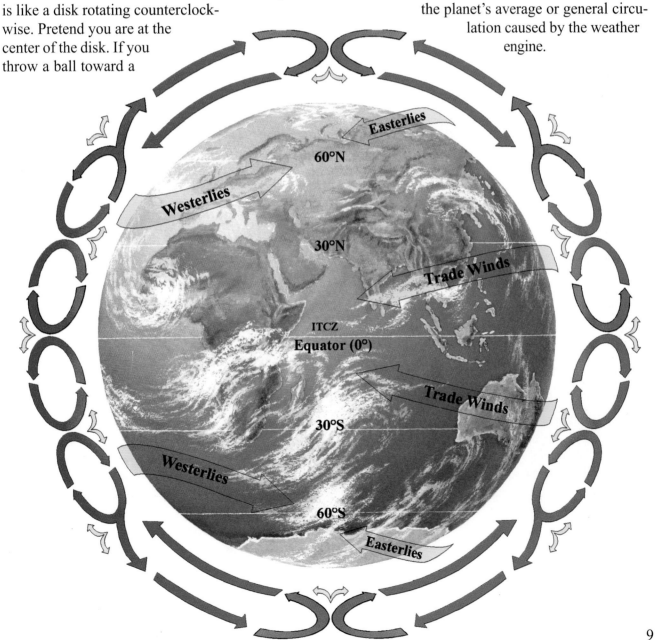

World Climate Zones

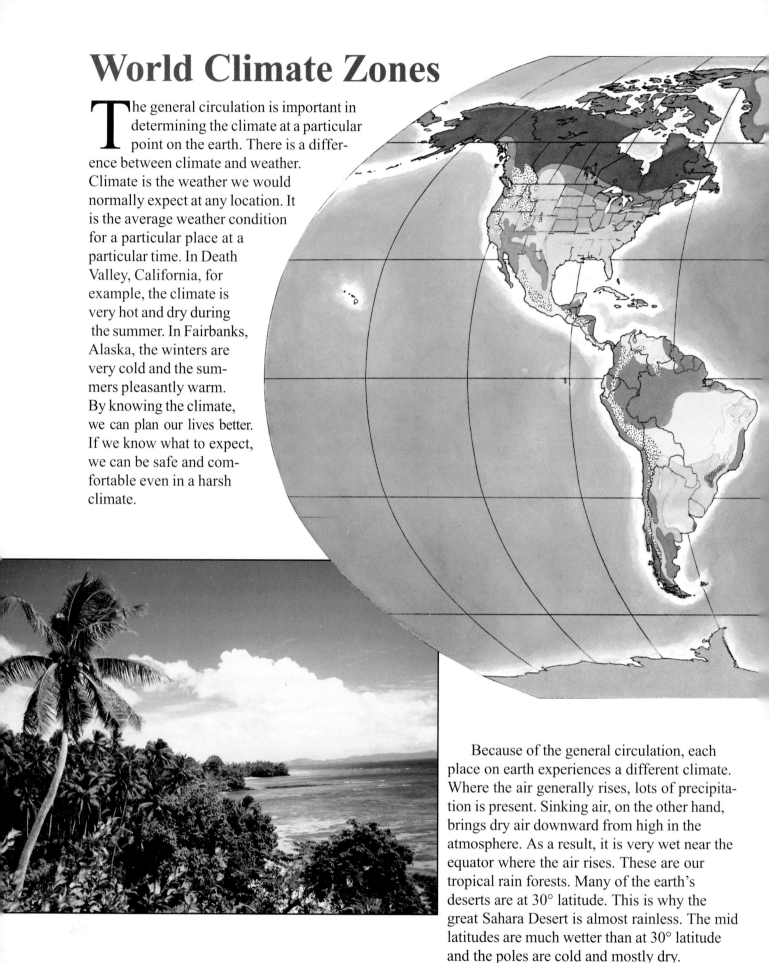

The general circulation is important in determining the climate at a particular point on the earth. There is a difference between climate and weather. Climate is the weather we would normally expect at any location. It is the average weather condition for a particular place at a particular time. In Death Valley, California, for example, the climate is very hot and dry during the summer. In Fairbanks, Alaska, the winters are very cold and the summers pleasantly warm. By knowing the climate, we can plan our lives better. If we know what to expect, we can be safe and comfortable even in a harsh climate.

Because of the general circulation, each place on earth experiences a different climate. Where the air generally rises, lots of precipitation is present. Sinking air, on the other hand, brings dry air downward from high in the atmosphere. As a result, it is very wet near the equator where the air rises. These are our tropical rain forests. Many of the earth's deserts are at 30° latitude. This is why the great Sahara Desert is almost rainless. The mid latitudes are much wetter than at 30° latitude and the poles are cold and mostly dry.

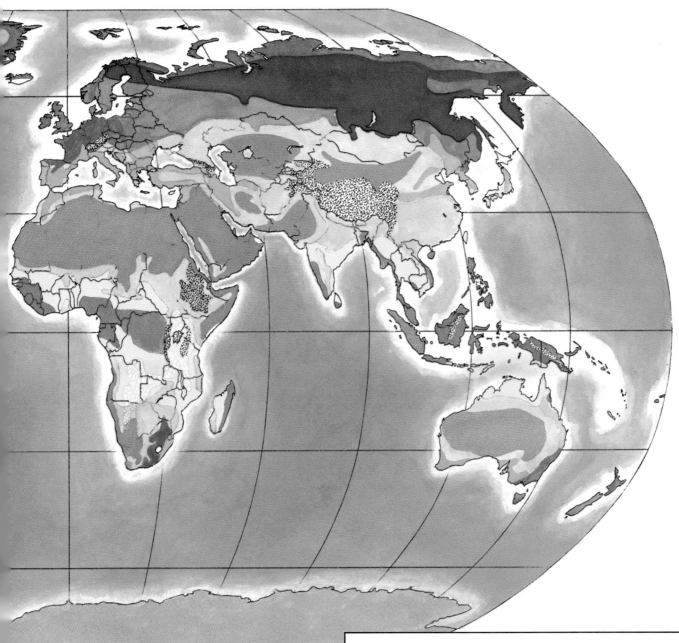

Other variables, in addition to the general circulation, help to determine climate. A main variable is distance from the ocean. The closer to the ocean, especially in the mid latitudes, the wetter the climate. The farther from the ocean, the drier. The presence of mountains is also another variable. Mountains are cooler and wetter. Upwind from a mountain range is wetter, while downwind it is drier. The general circulation, land-ocean distribution, and mountains all cause a complicated climate pattern.

World Climate

Tropical
- *Tropical Wet*
- *Tropical Wet & Dry*

Dry
- *Semiarid*
- *Arid*

Mild
- *Marine West Coast*
- *Mediterranean*
- *Humid Subtropical*

Continental
- *Warm Summer*
- *Cool Summer*
- *Subarctic*

Polar
- *Tundra*
- *Ice Cap*

High Elevations
- *Highlands*
- *Uplands*

11

Weather Facts

Hottest

The hottest temperature ever recorded was 136.4°F (58°C). This reading was taken in the shade at Azizia, Libya, September 13, 1922. Azizia is just north of the Sahara Desert.

Death Valley, California, is a close second. In 1913 it reached 134°F (56.7°C).

In 1889 Queensland, Australia, soared to 127.6°F (53.1°C).

The hottest place in the world is Dallol in Ethopia. It is on the edge of the Sahara Desert and has an *average* annual temperature of 93.3°F (34.4°C).

Death Valley.

Windiest

The highest recorded surface wind speed was a tornado in Texas. It was measured at 280 mph (450 kph).

On Mount Washington, in New Hampshire, a gust of wind was recorded at 231 mph (371 kph).

The George V Coast in Antarctica has recorded winds of 200 mph (320 kph).

Inside Mt. Waialeale crater on Kauai, Hawaii.
It rains 365 days a year.

Strangest

We've all heard the expression, "It's raining cats and dogs." Well, on June 16, 1939, in Trowbridge, England, it actually "rained" tiny frogs. Strong winds had picked them up from nearby ponds and they fell back to earth with the rain.

Wettest

Although Mt. Waialeale has the highest yearly average rainfall, 460 inches (1,168 cm) a year, Cherrapunji, India, holds the record for any one year. Cherrapunji is affected by the monsoon, so it receives much summer rainfall and little in the winter. During the month of July 1861 it rained 366.14 inches (930 cm); the total for the year was a whopping 905.12 inches (2,299 cm)!

The largest recorded amount of rain to fall in one day was 73.62 inches (187 cm) at Cilaos La Reunion. In the United States, Alvin, Texas, received 43 inches (109 cm) of rain in one day. That is more rain than most places in North America receive all year.

The largest amount of rainfall in one hour was 12 inches (30 cm) in Holt, Missouri, and at Kilauea Sugar Plantation, Hawaii.

Siberia.

Coldest

The coldest temperature ever recorded in the world was -129°F (-89°C). It was measured July 21, 1983, at Vostok on the Antarctic Ice Sheet at 11,200 feet (3,400 m) above sea level. At that temperature carbon dioxide can freeze to dry ice.

Siberia has the second coldest record. Their record low is only -90°F (-68°C). The coldest temperature ever recorded in North America was -81°F (-63°C) at Snag, Yukon Territory, Canada.

Did you know that fresh snow reflects about 90 percent of the solar radiation (heat and light energy) back into the atmosphere? The snow surface receives so little heat the air above it stays cold.

Lowest

The lowest air pressure on earth probably occurs at the center of a tornado. It is doubtful if it could ever be measured. It would be very difficult to place a barometer at the center, and if it could be done the winds would no doubt destroy it.

Typhoon Tip had the lowest air pressure ever recorded; it was 25.69 inches (65.3 cm) on October 12, 1979.

Deepest

The snowfall on Mt. Rainier, Washington, in the 1971–72 season was 93.5 feet (28.5 m) or 1,122 in. This is the U.S. snow season record.

In 1921, 6.3 feet (1.9 m) of snow fell at Silver Lake, Colorado, in just 24 hours.

London, England, recorded snowdrifts of 15 feet (4.6 m) in 1881.

Fastest

What was probably one of the fastest temperature changes happened in Spearfish, South Dakota, on January 22, 1943. At 7:30 in the morning the temperature rose 49°F (27°C) in just two minutes.

Driest

Two of the driest areas of the world are northern Chile and the eastern Sahara Desert. Most years they do not receive any rainfall. In fact, Calama, Chile, didn't have a drop of rain from 1570 to 1971. That's 400 years without rain!

Did you know that the top of the Antarctic ice sheet normally receives only an inch (2.5 cm) of water in the form of snow each year? In fact, it is called a polar desert. Remember that Antarctica is a continent of land layered with ice. Where do you think its 10,000 feet (3,050 m) of ice could have come from, if the precipitation is this low? (See pages 68–69.)

Adélie penguins basking in the Antarctic sunshine.

13

How to Read a Weather Map

If you watch the weather on TV or read a newspaper's weather report, you will usually see a weather map displayed. This map will have low and high pressure centers with lines drawn around them. Before the map can be drawn, however, weather observations at the same time must be taken from all over the earth.

There are two types of weather observations. One type is the surface observation. Each weather station takes measurements of temperature, dew point, clouds, precipitation, pressure, and wind speed and direction. These are sent out by computer to other stations at least once an hour. The second type of observation is the upper air observation. This is done by weather balloons and taken twice a day. The instrument on the balloon measures the temperature, dew point, and pressure in the atmosphere up to 100,000 feet (30,500 m). A special radar tracks the balloon and provides wind direction and speed. All these observations are then plotted on maps. Weather maps used to be drawn by hand but now computers draw them.

On a surface map, lines connecting stations with equal pressure are drawn. From these lines we find where the low pressure and high pressure centers are. On the map you will see the location of high pressure centers labeled with "H," and low pressure centers labeled with "L." High pressure areas are generally good weather areas, except in winter the temperatures may be cold, like in an Arctic high that moves southward from Canada or Alaska. Low pressure areas are generally areas of stormy weather.

You will also see weather fronts on the map. A front is a boundary between air of different temperature and moisture content. If the front is not moving it is called a stationary front and is shown by a line with alternating triangles and semicircles. If the cold air, which is usually to the north or west, is displacing the warm air, it is a cold front and is labeled by a line with triangles. The triangles are drawn pointing in the direction the cold air is moving. If warm air is pushing out cold air, it is a warm front. A warm front is shown

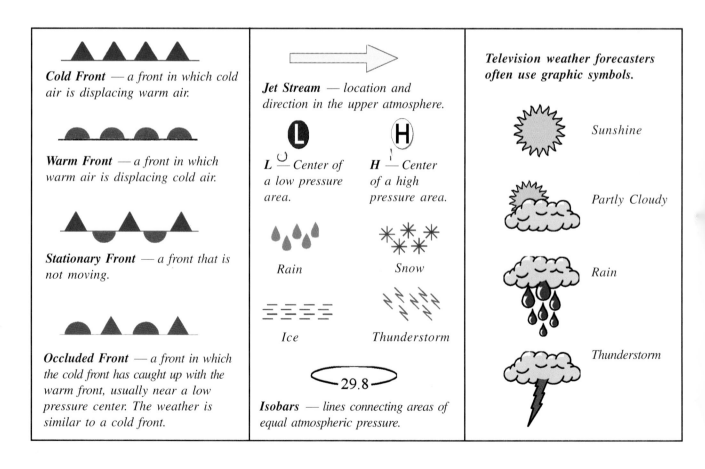

Cold Front — a front in which cold air is displacing warm air.

Warm Front — a front in which warm air is displacing cold air.

Stationary Front — a front that is not moving.

Occluded Front — a front in which the cold front has caught up with the warm front, usually near a low pressure center. The weather is similar to a cold front.

Jet Stream — location and direction in the upper atmosphere.

L ⌣ Center of a low pressure area.

H ˙ Center of a high pressure area.

Rain

Snow

Ice

Thunderstorm

Isobars — lines connecting areas of equal atmospheric pressure. 29.8

Television weather forecasters often use graphic symbols.

Sunshine

Partly Cloudy

Rain

Thunderstorm

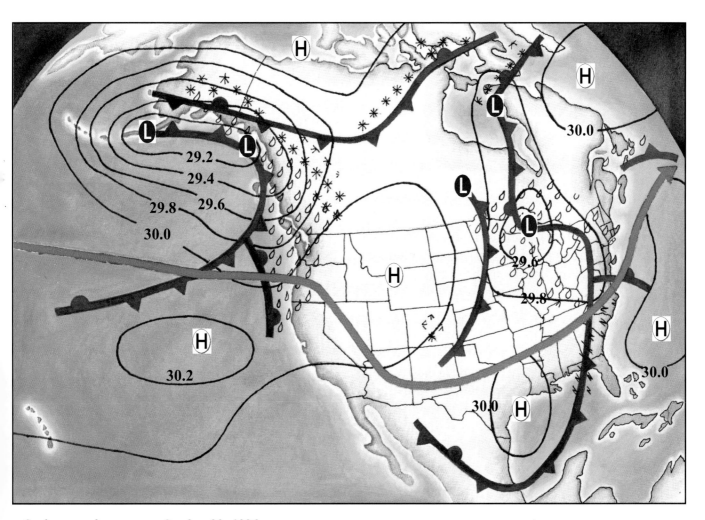

Surface weather map on October 23, 1996.

by a line with semicircles, the rounded part pointing in the direction of movement, which is usually northward.

Using weather observations, the locations of all the fronts on a weather map, and the jet stream, the weatherperson can now make a forecast. From studying the atmosphere and the many scientific processes that occur, meteorologists have developed equations. These equations are fed into one of the world's fastest computers and projected into the future. After millions of computer operations, the position of the jet stream, the fronts, and the pressure centers are estimated in the future. This information is plotted on forecast maps at big weather centers and sent all over the world to smaller weather stations.

The weatherperson at each weather station receives lines on a map that represent the future weather pattern. He or she must then interpret

these lines for their area. Over the years weather maps have improved. They are not perfect, however. Meteorologists do not know enough about the atmosphere, nor do they have enough observations. They need bigger and faster computers. So the weather maps still have to be interpreted. Even if the weather maps were perfect, it would be difficult to forecast the exact weather for their specific area. A weatherperson works from lines on the map, radar, and satellite pictures to predict temperature, precipitation, wind, and cloud conditions. They also issue advisories, watches, and warnings. Many times forecasting is easy; sometimes it is difficult. That explains why weather forecasts are sometimes incorrect.

Memory Tip: A science teacher in southern California taught his students how to remember the difference between a cold and warm front. Think of the triangles as icicles and the semicircles as blisters.

Jet Stream

The jet stream is a ribbon of high-speed wind in the upper atmosphere. It generally moves from a westerly direction at speeds that can exceed 250 mph (400 kph) at altitudes of 6 to 12 miles (10 to 20 km).

The weather engine causes the jet stream in the middle latitudes. The jet stream meanders around the globe like a snake. The Northern and Southern Hemispheres each have a jet stream. Many important weather features are connected to the jet stream.

The jet stream is caused by the difference in temperature between the tropical and polar latitudes. This temperature difference causes the west wind to increase upward. The wind reaches a maximum just below the stratosphere (an upper level of the atmosphere). The stronger the temperature difference between equator and pole, the stronger the wind. That is why the average speed of the jet stream is 90 mph (144 kph) during the winter and only 35 mph (56 kph) during summer.

Jet Stream Zigzags

The jet stream is constantly changing. The three globes below show the jet stream of the Northern Hemisphere at different times. The jet stream zigzags around the earth as waves. When the wind is strong, it often forms three waves. When the wind is weak, five waves are often observed. Sometimes the jet stream will split in two and reform downstream. To further complicate matters, the waves can remain stationary or they can move east or west. All these changes in the jet stream make forecasting the weather a challenge!

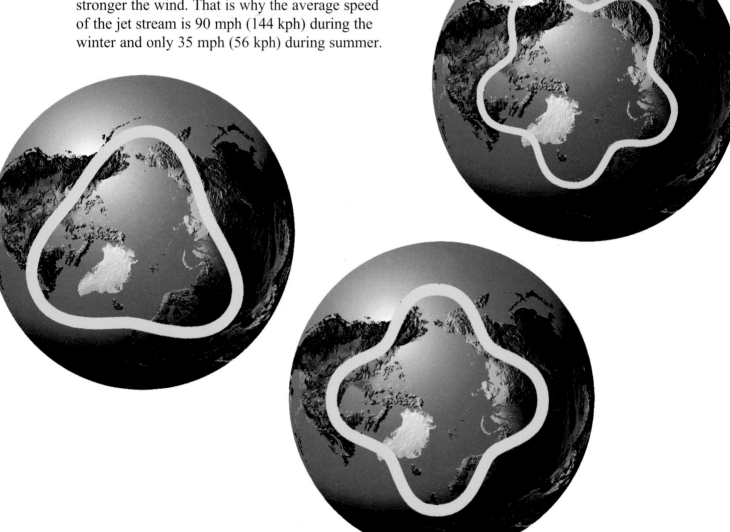

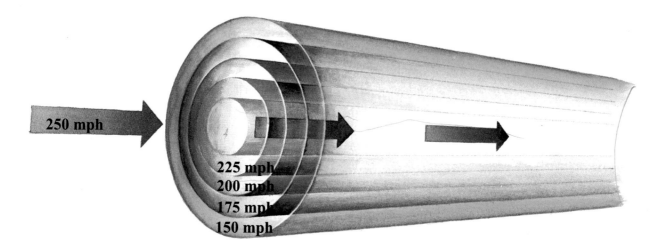

250 mph

225 mph
200 mph
175 mph
150 mph

In the illustrations to the left you will notice that the jet stream is made up of waves. Within one wave, the southwest wind transports warmer air north. The northwest wind transports colder air southward. This interaction causes a storm or a low pressure center. The storm is usually found below the southwest wind of the jet stream. The high pressure area is generally located below the northwest wind. Associated with the storm are cold and warm fronts. The storm is guided by the jet stream's wind direction. This is why storms generally move from west to east.

Wind speed within the jet stream also varies. It may blow 75 mph (120 kph) in one area, but further along it may blow 200 mph (320 kph). Meteorologists often think of the jet stream as a thick ribbon or a tube of air. They will draw wind speeds on a map of the world. The more lines in the tube the faster the air. Jet stream charts are important to weatherpersons because stormy weather can usually be found associated with certain portions of the maximum wind. If you placed a balloon in the jet stream, it would zigzag north and south, slow down and speed up. During all this commotion, the balloon would still make it around the world in about 14 days.

Surface map on October 9, 1996

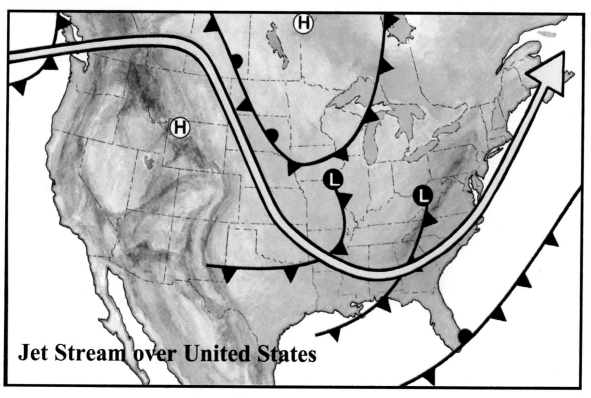

Jet Stream over United States

El Niño

The weather changes practically every day, but under special atmospheric and oceanic conditions small climate changes occur, too. These changes last only a year or two, but cause dramatic weather effects. One small, natural climatic change is called El Niño.

Normal

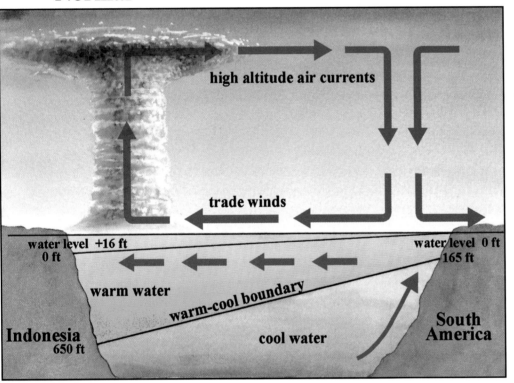

high altitude air currents

trade winds

water level +16 ft
0 ft

water level 0 ft
165 ft

warm water

warm-cool boundary

cool water

Indonesia
650 ft

South America

A cold ocean current, called the Peru current, flows northward along the South American coast of Peru and Ecuador. This water is cold because part of it comes from the deep ocean up to the surface. Deep ocean water contains generous amounts of food for plankton (small plant and animal organisms). The plankton multiply and become food for fish, which the local fishermen catch. This current is caused mostly by winds in the tropical atmosphere. Each year the current changes direction and becomes warmer for a while. The warming normally occurs around Christmas and that is why the current is called El Niño, which is Spanish for "the boy" or "Christ child." Early the next year the current usually changes direction and becomes cold again.

This sequence normally occurs every year. The people of Peru and Ecuador expect it. Usually, the change does not affect the weather very much. However, every two to seven years the warmer current becomes much warmer than normal. The warm water condition lasts from 18 to 24 months. The warmer water comes from the tropical ocean around Indonesia and the Philippine Islands. The warm water is poor in nutrients, so there are few plankton and, therefore, few fish. The fisherman's life becomes very difficult. The strongest recorded El Niño was in 1982 and 1983. Ocean temperatures rose 7 to 12°F (4 to 7°C) above normal off Peru. When the ocean and atmosphere return to a more normal pattern, El Niño changes to La Niña, the Spanish term for "the girl."

El Niño not only affects fishing off the Peruvian coast, but it also changes the weather in Peru and Ecuador. Usually their climate is similar to that of a desert. However, El Niño brings heavy rains and flooding. These changes occur because rainfall is closely tied to the ocean temperature. The warmer water of El Niño evaporates more water into the atmosphere. This water vapor is carried over land and develops into thunderstorms. The 1982–83 El Niño caused catastrophic flooding and mud slides.

It is well established that El Niño causes climate changes in the Pacific Ocean all around the equator. El Niño likely causes dry weather or drought in India, southeast Africa, and northern South America. Scientists have also thought it may be responsible for climate changes in other parts of the world as far away as northwest North America. These climate changes last for a season or up to a year. Scientists also believe that El Niño causes the southern United States to be wetter than normal in winter.

North America's connection with El Niño is not as strong as that of Peru and Ecuador because it is further from the tropical Pacific Ocean than the two South American coastal countries. However, there does appear to be a link. The warmer atmosphere near the equator in the Pacific Ocean causes the upper winds to be stronger at about 30° north latitude. During the winter these winds blow in an easterly direction over the ocean, moving storms into California. The storms continue moving eastward through the southern United States. The changed storm track causes the northwest United States and British Columbia, Canada, to be drier than normal. The last several El Niño episodes have caused mild, dry winters in Washington, Oregon, Idaho, Montana, and British Columbia.

Many variables affect weather changes, so the link may not be a strong one. The 1993 El Niño is thought by some scientists to have caused the terrible summer midwest floods in the United States. These are floods that occur only once every 200 to 500 years. Yet, the 1993 El Niño was not very strong. Then how could it cause all these dramatic climatic effects? Other variables are suspected, so research scientists continue to look for them.

Scientists still have much to learn about El Niño. They do not know what causes an El Niño, and much research is being done to find out. Recently they discovered that an El Niño-like event occurs in the Indian Ocean. The scientists also believe that the two El Niños have a powerful impact on global weather. The Indian Ocean El Niño occurs simultaneously with the Pacific El Niño. As warmer waters move from the east coast of Africa to India over a 12- to 18-month period, western Australia, Indonesia, and India experience droughts. So far, the research indicates that El Niños can change the climate for a year or two over the tropics and possibly in North America. The combined influence of the Pacific and Indian Ocean El Niños may extend even farther than is currently known, and that's what research scientists are trying to find out.

El Niño

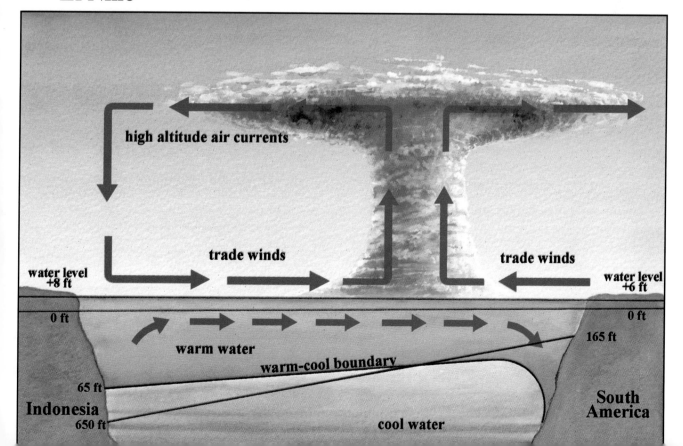

high altitude air currents

trade winds

trade winds

water level +8 ft

water level +6 ft

0 ft

0 ft

165 ft

warm water

warm-cool boundary

65 ft

Indonesia

650 ft

cool water

South America

Chapter 3
Water in the Atmosphere
How God Recycles Water

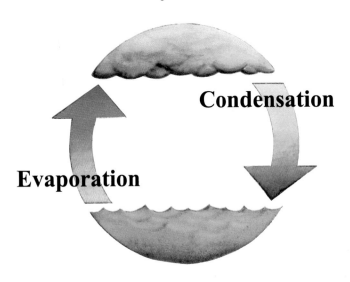

Condensation

Evaporation

In God's plan of creation He set up scientific processes that sustain His creation. These processes include the global water cycle.

Have you ever wondered where all the water for rain and snow comes from? About half of it comes from plants, wet ground, rivers, and lakes. You may be surprised to know the other half of our precipitation on land is evaporated from the ocean. The ocean covers about 70 percent of the earth — a lot of surface for evaporation to take place.

Evaporation occurs any time water is exposed to air. Leave a glass of water out overnight, and the next morning a small amount of the water will be gone. A better example of evaporation is when you take a hot shower. As warm water droplets spray into the cooler air, water evaporates from them. When the air in the room becomes filled with water vapor it forms clouds. This water then condenses on the cold mirrors and windows. When the condensation becomes heavy enough, it gathers into drops and runs down the glass. What happens in your bathroom is similar to how water drops evaporate and

condense to form clouds and rain. Evaporated ocean water is constantly being replaced by rain and by rainwater returning from the land by rivers and streams. This is called the water cycle or hydrological cycle. The cycle begins as vapor-laden air blows from the oceans to the land. The rain and snow fall on the land. Some of this precipitation is re-evaporated into the air. Rainwater that is not absorbed by the soil will run off into streams and rivers. Eventually, it empties once again into the ocean. If we could follow one water molecule, it would make a circle from the ocean to the land and then back to the ocean.

Rainwater that does not run toward the ocean soaks deep into the ground. This water feeds what we call the aquifer or water table. When the water table is

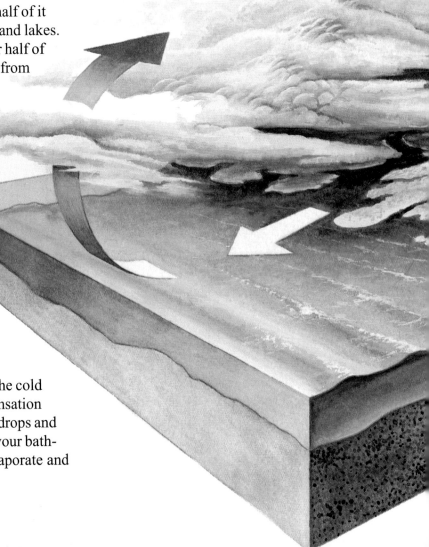

Evaporation.

abundantly supplied, it is high enough to provide water for wells and springs. Where the water table is deep in the ground, the land is dry.

Runoff from rainstorms picks up chemicals from the soil and carries them to the ocean. Small amounts of carbon, iron, phosphorus, nitrogen, and other chemicals are nutrients that sustain sea life. Microscopic marine plants and animals, called plankton, require these chemicals, along with photosynthesis (combining of chemical compounds aided by sunlight), to survive. Plankton is an essential food for many small marine creatures and even for baleen whales (they have whalebone plates for filtering plankton instead of teeth).

Through the water cycle, God provides life-sustaining water for man, animals, and plants. The run-off from the land to the ocean provides the nutrients necessary for marine plankton. These plankton are the beginning of the ocean food chain. In this way, the ocean will continue to have plentiful amounts of fish.

Water rushes toward the sea.

Clouds

The atmosphere always contains a little bit of invisible water vapor. Clouds form when the atmosphere can no longer hold all of the invisible water vapor. This happens when the air has reached 100 percent relative humidity. At this point, any extra water vapor condenses into very small water drops that float in the air, just like what happens in your bathroom when you take a shower. Warm air holds more water vapor than cool air. So if warm, moist air is cooled, it will form a cloud.

There are four different ways that moist air can be cooled enough to form clouds. It can be cooled by the ground at night from infrared radiation. This generates fog, which is really just a cloud that never rose.

Mountain clouds are formed when wind forces the air up a mountain ridge to where the air is cooler and water vapor condenses.

Convection clouds occur when solar radiation heats up the earth's surface and the heated air rises. As the warm air rises and cools, any water vapor condenses to form clouds.

Frontal clouds form when a wind blows warmer moist air into cooler air. When the warmer air collides with the cooler air, clouds are formed.

Mountain Cloud

Convection Cloud

Frontal Cloud

In 1803 an English pharmacist, Luke Howard, devised a system to put clouds into ten distinct categories. All of these are variations of the three main types on the next page. His system proved so reliable that meteorologists are still using it today.

3 Basic Cloud Types

Cumulus clouds are the white puffy clouds that look like cauliflower. Usually you see these fluffy white clouds on a bright, sunny day. They have flat bottoms but the tops are always changing shape.

A cumulus cloud means that the air is well mixed by up and down currents. When a cumulus cloud grows into a thunderstorm, the cloud is called a cumulonimbus cloud. This is a sign that the air is rising to the stratosphere.

Stratus clouds are low altitude gray clouds that form a rather flat base. The name comes from the Latin word *stratus*, which means to stretch or extend. You will see the best stratus clouds as thick cloud blankets near the ocean. They are occasionally called "high fogs." Light rain and drizzle often fall from stratus clouds. When precipitation falls from stratus clouds they are usually called nimbostratus.

Cirrus (sear-us) clouds are high altitude clouds that often form as high as 35,000 feet (over 10 km) and often look thin and feathery. They are composed of ice crystals instead of water drops. This is because the upper atmosphere is around -50°F (-45°C), even if it is warm on the ground. Thin cirrus clouds are sometimes called "mares' tails" because they can look like the tails of a horse. These are the first clouds you see when a warm front is approaching.

Elevation of Clouds

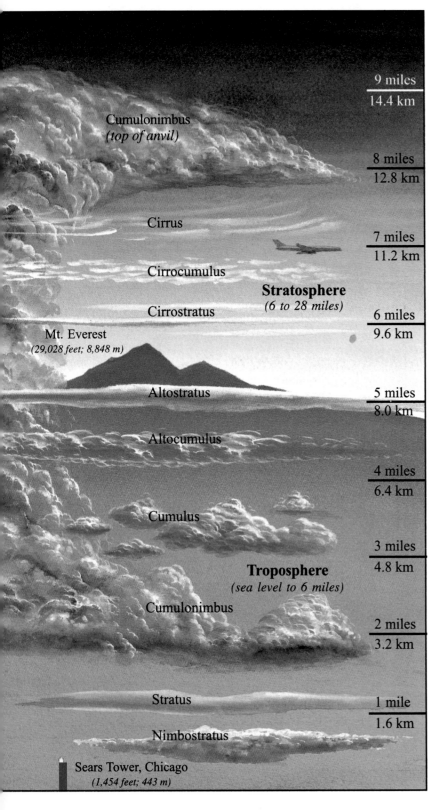

Cloud	Elevation
Cumulonimbus *(top of anvil)*	9 miles / 14.4 km
	8 miles / 12.8 km
Cirrus	7 miles / 11.2 km
Cirrocumulus	
Cirrostratus — **Stratosphere** *(6 to 28 miles)*	6 miles / 9.6 km
Mt. Everest *(29,028 feet; 8,848 m)*	
Altostratus	5 miles / 8.0 km
Altocumulus	4 miles / 6.4 km
Cumulus	3 miles / 4.8 km
Troposphere *(sea level to 6 miles)*	
Cumulonimbus	2 miles / 3.2 km
Stratus	1 mile / 1.6 km
Nimbostratus	
Sears Tower, Chicago *(1,454 feet; 443 m)*	

Cumulonimbus are tall cumulus clouds with a dark flat base. These thunderstorms often contain heavy rain showers and hail.

Cloud Classification

Clouds are classified according to their height in the sky.

High-level clouds are 20,000 feet (6,069 m) and up and are made of ice crystal. Their names start with *cirro* or *cirrus* (meaning curly).

Medium-level clouds are between 6,000 (1,829 m) and 20,000 feet. They are made up of water drops and ice crystals and their names start with *alto* (meaning high).

Low-level clouds range between ground level and 6,000 feet and are the *strato* clouds made of water drops.

Cumulo clouds are also low-level and are made up of water drops. When they push up through higher levels they contain ice crystals as well.

Lenticular (lens-shaped) clouds are one type of altocumulus clouds. They are formed by waves in moderate-to-strong winds on the leeward (away from the wind) side of mountains.

Nimbostratus are low gray stratus clouds with rain.

Stratocumulus are cumulus clouds that have spread horizontally to form broad sheets.

Cirrocumulus are tiny, high altitude clumps of shadowless cirrus clouds. They often form waves and ripples and are called a mackerel sky because they resemble the scales of a fish.

Cirrostratus are high cirrus clouds that have spread into a thin, milky sheet. Often the light shining through the ice crystals in the cloud forms a bright ring or halo, around the sun or moon.

Altostratus (above cumulus) is a thin sheet of clouds at medium heights that often cover the sky, making the sun look like it is shining through a frosted window.

Altocumulus are puffs and rolls of clouds at medium heights and often have dark shadows.

25

Warm Front

Cirrus clouds over mountain bluff.

God has provided several processes to cause water vapor in the atmosphere to condense into clouds. A warm front is one of these processes. A warm front is that part of the low pressure system in which warmer air pushes the colder air back. Warm fronts in the Northern Hemisphere mostly move from the south or west. Warm air is less dense than cold air. As warm air pushes against cold air, the warmer air rises above the colder air.

Most clouds and precipitation are formed in areas of rising air in the atmosphere. As the air rises, it cools, but the amount of water vapor remains fixed. Finally, the temperature cools to the point where water vapor condenses to form clouds. We see the same effect on a clear night when there is plenty of water vapor in the air. As the temperature falls, the water vapor condenses on objects such as cars and grass. Clouds form the same way. As the clouds continue to rise, the water droplets grow larger until they become heavy enough for gravity to pull them to the ground. The warm front causes the air to rise at an angle, and the rising air produces rain and snow.

We can tell when a warm front is approaching by the type of clouds observed. Because the warm front slants, the first clouds we see will be high clouds. As the warm front comes closer, the clouds become thicker and lower. Finally, close to the warm front the clouds are low and precipitation falls. After the warm front passes, the clouds usually decrease and the precipitation stops. Since most warm fronts move from west to east, sailors, farmers, and other people who depend upon the weather noticed the repeating pattern of clouds and precipitation. That

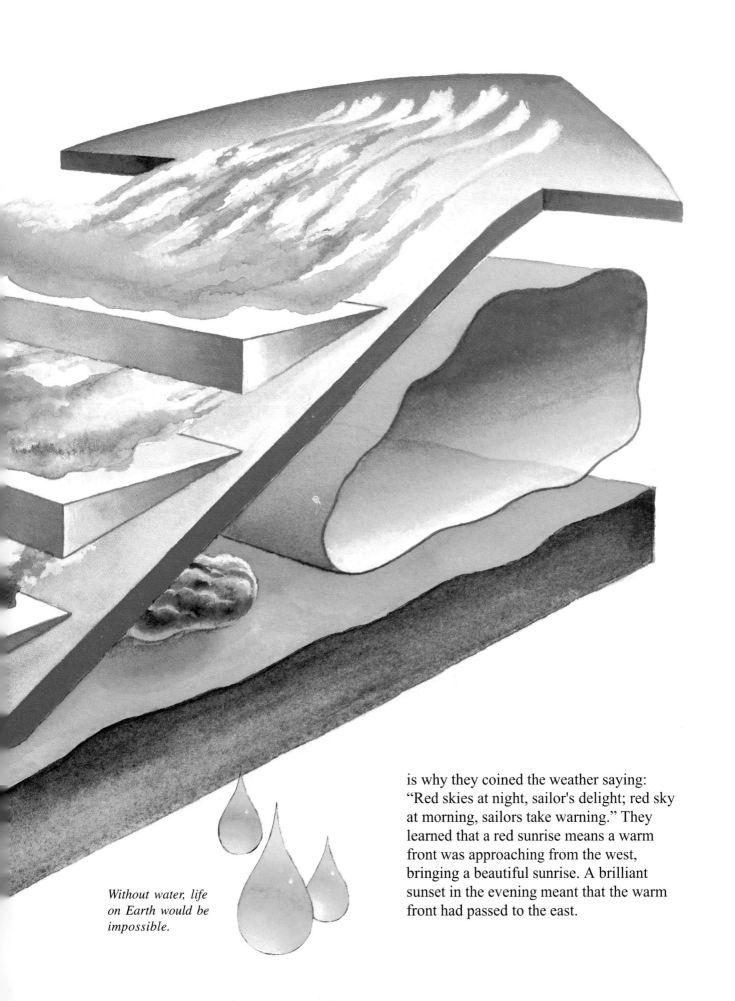

Without water, life on Earth would be impossible.

is why they coined the weather saying: "Red skies at night, sailor's delight; red sky at morning, sailors take warning." They learned that a red sunrise means a warm front was approaching from the west, bringing a beautiful sunrise. A brilliant sunset in the evening meant that the warm front had passed to the east.

Cold Front

God provided a second process in low pressure systems that causes rain and snow. This is the cold front, in which cold air replaces warm air. Since the cold air is usually north and northwest of a low pressure center, cold fronts most often come from the north or west. The colder air, being denser, dives underneath the warmer air. The less dense, warmer air is forced upward at a sharp angle. This rising air condenses and forms rain or snow.

Usually, the cold wind pushing the cold front from behind is much stronger than in warm fronts. Thus, cold fronts generally move faster than sluggish warm fronts. The fast motion causes the air to rise faster. In the warm season, rapidly rising air causes thunderstorms

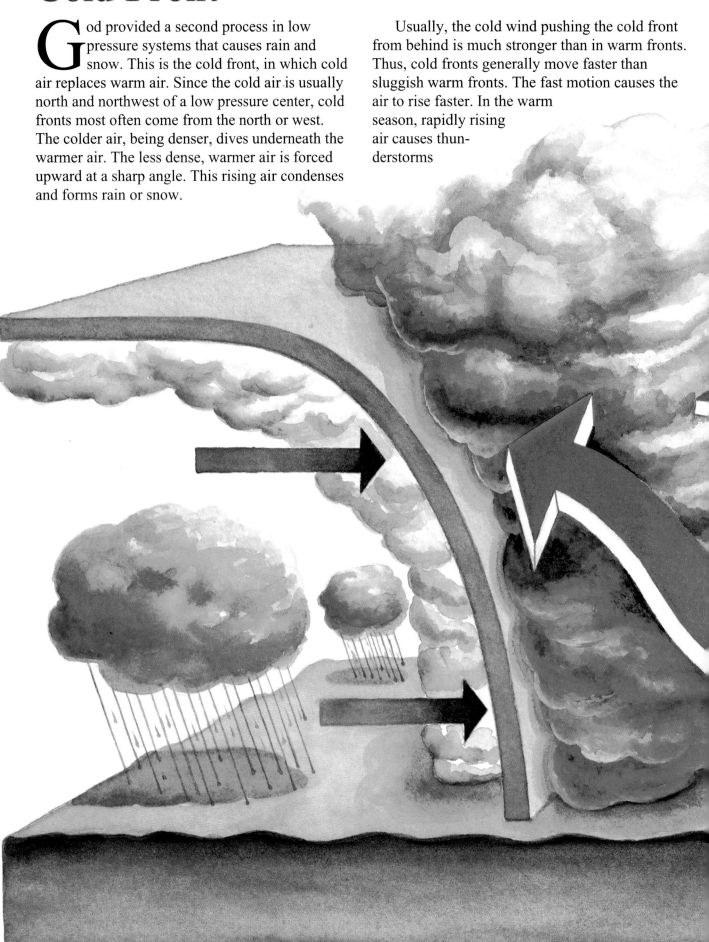

Cold front over Sacramento River.

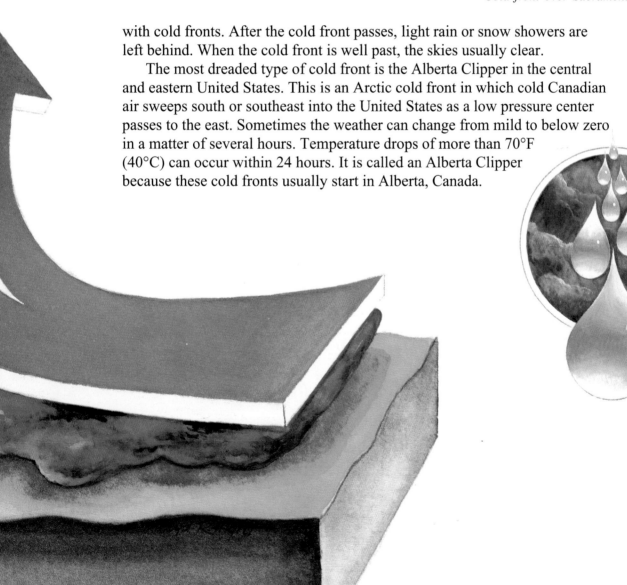

with cold fronts. After the cold front passes, light rain or snow showers are left behind. When the cold front is well past, the skies usually clear.

The most dreaded type of cold front is the Alberta Clipper in the central and eastern United States. This is an Arctic cold front in which cold Canadian air sweeps south or southeast into the United States as a low pressure center passes to the east. Sometimes the weather can change from mild to below zero in a matter of several hours. Temperature drops of more than 70°F (40°C) can occur within 24 hours. It is called an Alberta Clipper because these cold fronts usually start in Alberta, Canada.

Fog

Fog is essentially a cloud that forms on the ground. Fog can form in several ways. The most common way is on a clear night when the temperature drops and the relative humidity rises to 100 percent. At this point the water vapor in the air has to condense out as liquid drops. This type of fog is most common during the wintertime in many mountain valleys of the world. It can occur over the central and eastern United States most of the year. These areas can be quite moist, even in the summer, so it does not take much of a temperature drop at night to form fog.

Fog can form over water, usually at night. Evaporation into the air moistens the air till fog forms. This is called evaporation fog.

Another way for fog to form is for moist air to blow into cool air. In this way the cool air moistens up and the relative humidity increases until fog forms.

A third mechanism which forms fog occurs in mountainous or hilly terrain. Fog will occur when low clouds intersect the ground when trying to pass over high terrain. Sometimes fog will form even if moist air is uplifted over mountains. The clouds can form near the higher parts of the mountains. If you were up that high it would be fog to you.

In the western United States during winter, an inversion is usually present in many of the mountain valleys.

Dew Point

Moisture in the air condenses as it cools. As the air cools, it is able to hold less and less water. When the air can no longer hold any more water (point of saturation), it has reached its dew point. Water vapor condenses into droplets when it comes into contact with a cold surface.

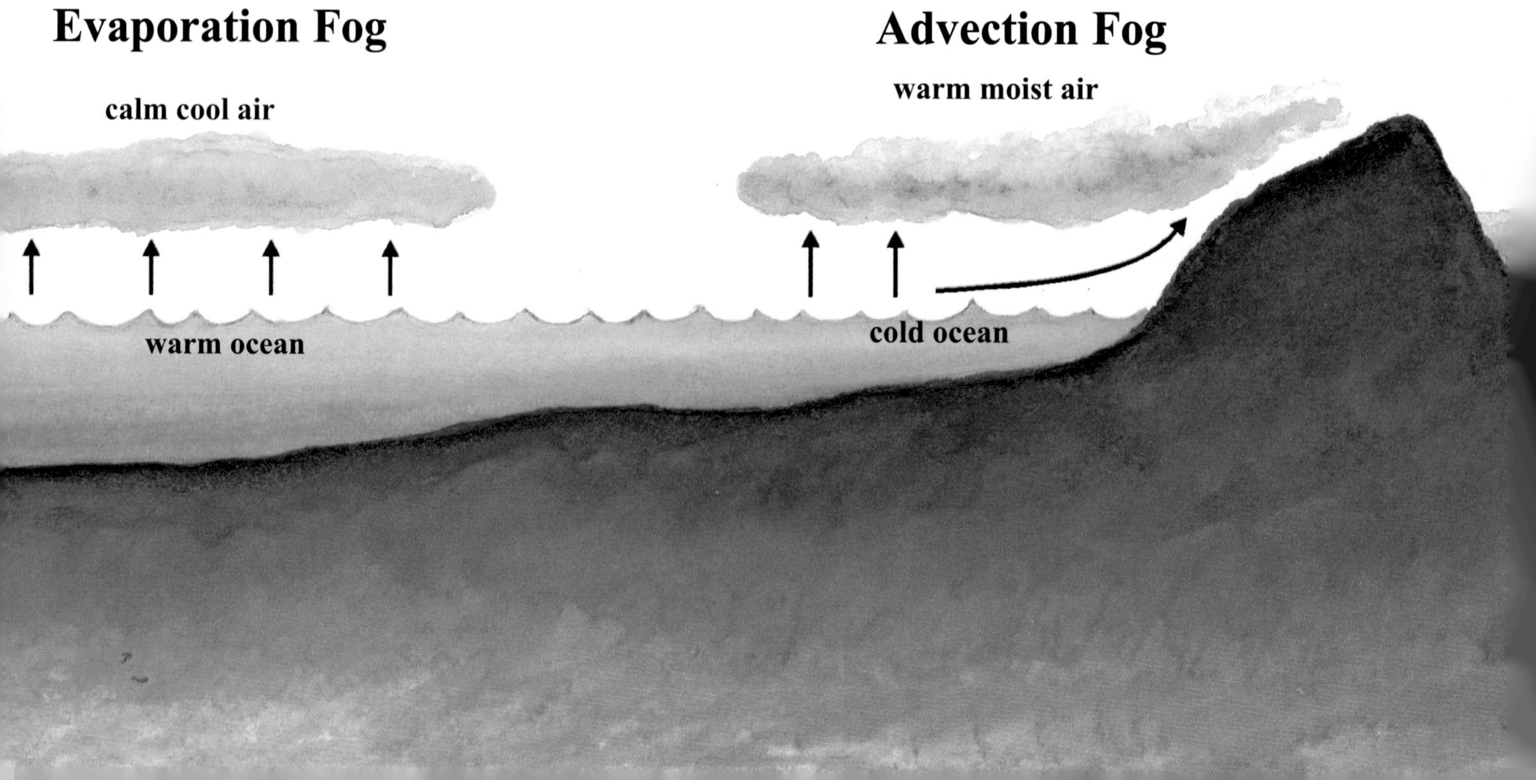

Evaporation Fog

calm cool air

warm ocean

Advection Fog

warm moist air

cold ocean

San Francisco Bay.

Yosemite Valley.

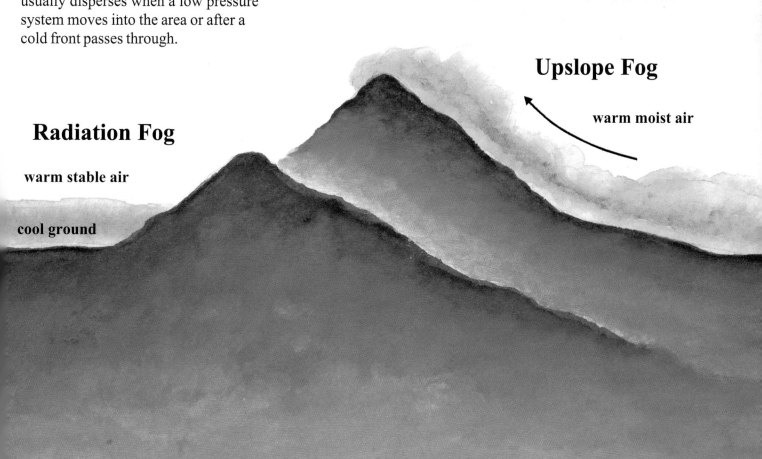

An inversion is where the temperature near the surface of the ground is colder than the air above it. If a stationary high pressure system is over the area, the fog can persist under the inversion for days. This is why fog can sometimes last for weeks in the San Juaquin and Sacramento Valleys of California. The fog in these valleys is called Tule fog. It usually disperses when a low pressure system moves into the area or after a cold front passes through.

Upslope Fog

warm moist air

Radiation Fog

warm stable air

cool ground

Chapter 4
Thunderstorms

A beautiful summer sun disappears as a line of dark clouds approach. You've heard distant rumbling for a while and watched as the winds blew the storm in your direction. Soon thunder crashes and jagged bolts of lightning pierce the sky. You run for cover just before the downpour hits. After a dramatic drum roll, clouds heavy with water release their payload. Rain pelts down in huge drops, depositing as much as one hundred million gallons of water within an hour. It comes so quickly that much of it runs off into gutters beside the road. In the

country it rushes through gullies and into swelling streams. The storm lasts only an hour or so; then the sun bursts forth. The summer thunderstorm moves on, leaving the earth smelling moist and fresh once again.

A thunderstorm releases an immense amount of electrical power in a small area of about one hundred square miles. In only 20 minutes, power from one thunderstorm can produce a week's worth of electricity for a large city. Across the earth, 100 lightning bolts strike every second. At any one moment, about 1,800 thunderstorms

occur around the earth. That adds up to 16 million a year worldwide. Approximately one hundred thousand of these thunderstorms take place annually in the United States alone.

Most of the world's thunderstorms occur in the tropics. For example, central Africa and Indonesia have storms nearly every day. Imagine living in Kampala, Uganda, where 242 thunderstorms strike each year! Kampala is believed by experts to hold the world's record for thunderstorms in a year. Most of the storms in North America occur in the southeast.

Thunderstorms develop from fluffy cumulus clouds. A gentle cumulus cloud can suddenly mushroom into a giant thunderstorm — a cumulonimbus cloud. Three conditions are necessary to make this dramatic change. The first is a large difference in temperature between the ground and upper troposphere. The second requirement is

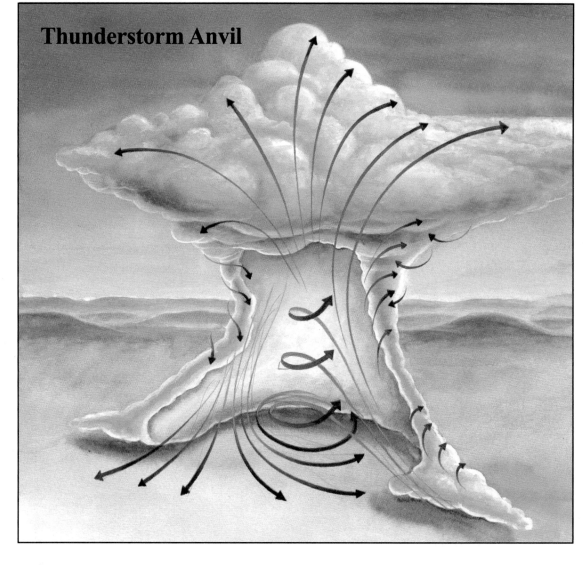

Thunderstorm Anvil

plenty of moisture in the lower atmosphere. A third condition is a trigger — a process to start the thunderstorm. Once such a storm is triggered, the moisture and temperature differences cause strong winds to blow upward from the ground. These winds are called updrafts.

Usually there are more clouds in the afternoon than in early morning. This is because the ground has warmed up enough by the afternoon for updrafts to develop. If there is very little moisture, an updraft has to go much higher before the water vapor condenses into a cloud. Sometimes the air will rise as high as 5,000 to 10,000 feet (1,524 to

3,048 m) before a little cumulus cloud condenses from the invisible water vapor.

High puffy little clouds do not change until a large amount of moisture is added. This moisture strengthens the updraft. Moisture adds heat, which means the cloud will warm inside and rise even faster. The moisture causes the cumulus cloud to mushroom upward and transform into a huge towering cumulus. The winds inside this cloud are very strong. Sometimes the updraft will reach 60 mph (96 kph). Thunder and lightning usually start when the top of the cloud reaches about 25,000 feet (7,620 m). The inside of the cloud by this time is cold enough that the water drops are turned into ice crystals. A cumulus cloud stops growing when it hits the stratosphere, a warmer layer of air in

thunderstorm weakens in the group, another grows. Because the ground usually cools off at night, thunderstorms normally don't last past sunset. Sometimes, though, the ground temperature remains warm all night. On a hot summer evening, the storms continue on into the night until the ground cools. Also, if a low pressure system is in the area, thunderstorms can occur at night.

Overall, thunderstorms are a great blessing to man and all living creatures. They are the main source of water for the interior of mid-latitude continents during the summer. Plants receive an

the upper atmosphere. Some thunderstorms grow twice as high as Mount Everest. Strong upper winds in the stratosphere brush off the top of the cloud and spread it. This makes the cloud resemble the top of a mushroom or an anvil. The ice crystals in the anvil cloud give it a fuzzy look. An anvil is a block of metal a blacksmith hammers against when shaping horseshoes. As a thunderstorm develops, water drops or ice crystals inside the cloud grow by colliding and merging with each other. The bottom of the cloud grows dark with water waiting to fall. When the drops become so heavy that the winds inside the cloud cannot sweep them up any more, they fall from the cloud as rain or hail. Even as they fall the water drops grow by combining with the smaller drops. This produces huge splashing raindrops. Hail gains its size inside the cloud. The falling hail and raindrops start a downdraft that eventually interferes with the moist updraft and weakens the thunderstorm. One thunderstorm cloud usually runs out of energy within 30 to 50 minutes.

Usually, thunderstorms come in a large group. One marches behind the other. So, as one

abundance of life-sustaining rainfall when they need it the most. Without the thunderstorms, these continents would become parched and dry. Fish would die, crops would fail, and animals would perish. Thunderstorms provide water for most of the world's food.

Thunderstorms provide other benefits we often take for granted. They are natural air conditioners. Heated air at the surface rises upward into the high atmosphere where it is released into space. Cloud formation provides shade. Rain and hail bring refreshing cooling after a hot day. Thunderstorms act collectively like a thermostat to keep the earth as a whole from becoming too hot. Without this upward heat pump, the earth

nitrogen fertilizer needed for farming is provided by lightning.

So, despite the dangers of lightning, thunderstorms are a blessing to us. They provide summer water, cool the earth, and clean the air. Lightning balances the earth's electricity and helps fertilize the soil. Lightning and thunderstorms are part of God's plan for protecting life on earth. Rainbows sometimes are seen with thunderstorms. The sun shines through drops of falling rain, causing the light to split into a spectrum of colors. This is a reminder of God's promise to never flood the whole earth again.

would be as much as 20°F (11°C) warmer. Thunderstorms also are one of God's air cleaners. During the summer, dust, haze, and other pollutants collect in the lower atmosphere. Rising air, either in cumulus clouds or in thunderstorms, spreads the pollution higher in the atmosphere. Rain from thunderstorms washes many of these particles out of the air.

Lightning in thunderstorms serves a purpose as well. It helps maintain the electrical balance of the earth and atmosphere. Lightning also forms fertilizer. When it splits the sky, lightning changes nitrogen gas in the air into nitrogen compounds. These, in turn, fall to the earth and are added to the soil. Nitrogen is one of the main ingredients in fertilizer. Ten percent of the

Safety Tips

- If lightning approaches seek shelter in a house, car or low area under some small trees, but not in a shed. Inside a house, do not use the telephone or any appliance. Do not bathe or take a shower.
- Stay away from water.
- Do not stand on a hilltop. Avoid being the tallest object.
- Do not seek shelter under an isolated tree.
- Stay away from metal pipes, fences, and wire clotheslines.
- If your hair stands on end while outside, immediately drop to the ground and curl into a ball.

Lightning

You might have wondered what causes lightning. In 1772, Benjamin Franklin was the first to demonstrate that a thunderstorm generates electricity. Lightning is like the static electricity you experience when you rub your foot on a rug and touch a doorknob. Your foot rubs electrons from the rug that travel through you to your finger tips. A spark of electricity shoots from your finger to the doorknob. In a thunderstorm the lower cloud becomes charged with as much as 100 million volts of electricity. This electricity is discharged either within the cloud, to the ground, to another cloud, or even into the air. Lightning has even been known to travel from the ground upwards to the cloud. In 1993 scientists discovered lightning bolts that shot upward from the top of a cumulonimbus cloud.

Scientists are still trying to understand lightning. Many scientists think that lightning is formed when electricity builds up in the cloud as a result of ice particles colliding. Negative electrons rub off onto larger ice particles. These crystals are so heavy they descend to the lower part of the cloud. The smaller ice crystals become positively charged and rise to the top of the cloud in the powerful updrafts. This process separates the negative charges from the positive charges. This separation causes a large difference in voltage between the bottom and the top of the cloud, and between the ground and the cloud bottom. Since opposite charges attract, the voltage difference becomes so large that a huge spark pierces the air. The electrons shoot to the area of the positive charge, either to the ground or up into the cloud.

There are many problems with this theory. Scientists have shown that even small cumulus clouds can generate electricity. They have also

Which Way Does Lightning Travel?

Electrical charges build up in the cloud. Positive (+) at the top, and negative (-) at the bottom.

Leader stroke discharges the negative charge in the cloud into the positively charged ground.

Return stroke flashes up from the ground, heating the air. The air expands with a clap of thunder.

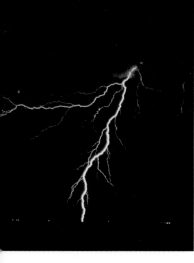

found that electricity can form without ice crystals. Sometimes, high amounts of electricity flow from the air into the cloud. Since, in most cases, the bottom of the cloud is negatively charged with electrons, cloud to ground lightning usually is negatively charged. But, 2 to 3 percent of these lightning bolts are not negative electrons, but positive charges. The positively charged bolts are the most dangerous. Scientists cannot explain how lightning is positively charged. Nature is very complex, and there is still much we need to learn about it.

Thunder is created when a lightning bolt splits the air. It heats the surrounding air molecules to 50,000°F (28,000°C) within a few millionths of a second. That is five times the temperature of the sun's surface. This explosive temperature rise causes the air to expand violently. This expansion generates thunder. Sound is caused by vibrations or waves in the air that your ear picks up. A way to demonstrate sound is to feel the vibrations of a lower sound played through a "subwoofer" speaker. It makes the room rumble.

Sound echoes and, therefore, you hear it differently when it is close rather than when it is far away. When lightning is near it sounds like a sharp crack. But when it is farther away it makes a rumbling noise. The rumble is caused by sound waves bouncing off objects, forming echoes.

You might think that thunder and lightning happen at the same time, since the sound waves explode at the same time as the lightning bolts. But they don't. Thunder travels at the speed of sound, which is 750 mph (1,200 kph). Lightning travels at the speed of light, a million times faster than the speed of sound. You can calculate how many miles the thunderstorm is from you by counting the number of seconds between the

lightning and the thunder. Then divide the seconds by five. Thunder normally can be heard up to seven miles (11 km) away. On a quiet day a person might hear a faint rumble from 20 miles (32 km) away.

Chapter 5
Dangerous Thunderstorms

Although most thunderstorms just bring brief heavy rain and moderate winds, some are ferocious. Of the 100,000 thunderstorms that occur in the United States each year, one out of ten brings damaging winds, large hail, tornadoes, and flash floods. These often injure and kill people and destroy crops and homes.

People often wonder why a God as wonderful as ours would allow dangerous thunderstorms. There is no simple answer for each event, especially if someone is badly hurt. But, the Bible says that all nature groans for God's redemption. Nature is a little out of whack as the result of sin after Adam and Eve rebelled against God. Yet, even dangerous storms can give us a hint of God's power. God gives mankind the knowledge and ability to predict dangerous weather patterns so we can protect ourselves. This is one of His provisions for us.

Regular thunderstorms develop when warm air near the ground combines with moist air causing an updraft. A severe thunderstorm requires both a strong updraft and a strong downdraft. A strong updraft is formed under three conditions: (1) when the ground is extra warm, (2) the air is extra moist, and (3) the air above is extra cool. The stronger the updraft, the more violent the thunderstorm.

When large raindrops or hail form in the strong updraft, they produce a strong downdraft as they fall. Severe thunderstorm downdrafts become even stronger when there is dry air 6,000 to 12,000 feet (2 to 4 km) above the ground.

Many countries experience severe thunderstorms. However, the United States experiences the most severe thunderstorms because of its geography. During spring and summer in the United States, extra moist air blows northward from the Gulf of Mexico over the well-heated plains. The extra moisture comes from the warm water of the Gulf of Mexico. Water evaporates more quickly in warm water than cold water, and warm air holds more water vapor than cool air. The combination of warm earth and moist air creates thunderstorms. This powerful combination generates the severe thunderstorms in the United States. Most of these occur in the southern and central midwest.

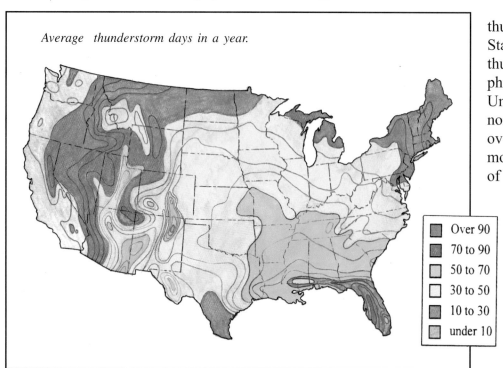

Average thunderstorm days in a year.

■	Over 90
■	70 to 90
□	50 to 70
□	30 to 50
■	10 to 30
■	under 10

This area stretches from Texas north into Nebraska and east into Missouri. Because the Gulf of Mexico's moisture moves east, the eastern United States has more severe thunderstorms than west of the Rockies or the northern Midwest.

causing a rush of water to roar downstream. Flash floods can also happen when it rains heavily on rapidly melting snow.

If thunderstorms are in the area, stay out of low places like gullies or stream beds. Cars should not be driven through water that is flowing over a road or bridge. Shallow, swiftly flowing water can wash a car off a roadway. It only takes two feet of water to float most cars. Worse yet, the road under the water may already have been washed out, leaving a deep hole. A flash flood can easily overturn a car, van, or recreational vehicle and trap its occupants. If your car stalls in flood waters, you must get out as fast as possible and go to higher ground. Nearly half the people who die in flash floods in the United States die in automobiles.

Flash floods occur when slow-moving thunderstorms drop an unusual amount of water on a small area. It rains so hard the water can not soak into the ground. The longer it rains, the greater the chance of a flash flood, and the more severe the flood will become. The water rushes down the mountainsides or hills into the streams and rivers. These streams and rivers cannot carry all the water, so it quickly floods. The most severe flash floods cause the water level to rapidly rise to dangerous levels in streams, dry washes, or canyons. They can also trigger catastrophic mud slides. Flash floods move at incredible speeds and have been known to roll big boulders, tear out trees, and destroy buildings and bridges.

Flash floods also occur when two or more gully-washing thunderstorms hit the same spot, one right after the other. They can occur when a dam bursts or an ice or debris jam breaks up,

Even though people who live in flash flood areas are well aware of the danger, there are always those who choose to ignore the warnings and often have to be rescued later.

Hail and Wind Damage

Have you ever seen hail the size of a golf ball? You may have, especially if you live in the Midwest of the United States. For a thunderstorm to be considered severe, the hail needs to be only 3/4 inch (1.9 cm) in diameter, the size of a dime. About 5,000 hailstorms a year in the United States produce hail 3/4 of an inch or larger.

A hailstone begins as an innocent little water drop or a round snow pellet in a cloud. The drop has already grown by collecting a million cloud droplets. The little drop is blown by a strong updraft inside the cloud to where it meets with some supercooled water drops. These supercooled drops are still liquid water even though the temperature is below freezing. When the little drop collides with these supercooled drops they join company. The little drop has now become a hailstone. The little hailstone is tossed up inside the cloud, all the while collecting other supercooled drops. The hailstone gets larger and larger until it reaches the top of the cloud. Then it runs out of updraft and falls back down through the cloud. On the way down it gets even bigger as it bangs into more supercooled drops. If it ends up in a very fast downdraft it can hit the earth at up to 90 mph (144 kph), bouncing like popcorn. If the hailstone hits soil, it can bury itself. It is fun to watch, but from under cover. Large hail can sting, bruise, or tear your skin. If it is extra big, your life could be in danger.

The stronger the updraft in the cumulonimbus cloud, the larger the hail. The stronger updrafts take the cumulonimbus cloud so high that the water drop has to travel very far before it reaches the top of the cloud. The farther it has to travel up and then down, the more opportunities it has to join with other supercooled drops. It takes ten billion cloud droplets to form a golf ball-sized hailstone.

The largest hailstone ever documented in the United States (photo at right) weighed 1.67 pounds (.75 of a kilogram) and was 5.5 in. (14 cm) across. It fell near Coffeyville, Kansas, on September 3, 1970. The largest verified hailstone in the world weighed 4.2 pounds, or almost 2 kilograms. It fell in Kazakhstan in central Asia.

Hailstones are made of alternating rings of clear and cloudy ice. The rings represent different rates of freezing on the hailstone. The cloudy ice is caused mainly by rapid

Hail forms in the strong wind currents of cumulonimbus clouds

Severe thunderstorms also cause wind damage. For a thunderstorm to be considered severe in the United States, it has to produce winds of 58 mph (93 kph) or greater. The wind speed rule may vary a little in other countries, but essentially is the lowest wind speed that begins to cause damage. The wind in some severe thunderstorms, however, can gust to more than 100 mph (160 kph). Winds this powerful can cause a

freezing, trapping many small air bubbles. The clear ring is caused by slow freezing of the water, which allows the bubbles to escape.

Hail normally lasts only a few minutes. But on June 3, 1959, a hailstorm in Selden, Kansas, lasted 85 minutes and covered the town 18 inches deep. Sometimes the wind blows hail into drifts up to three feet deep. At other times hail falls with no wind. Hail is mostly round, but sometimes it comes in strange shapes. Some hailstones have ragged edges like quartz crystals.

Hail does a tremendous amount of damage every year. Hail damage occurs in swaths, up to a hundred miles long and a few miles wide. It causes about 2 billion dollars in crop losses in North America alone each year. Even small hail with strong winds can mow down a field of wheat within minutes. Hail can severely dent cars, roofs, and siding. It sometimes breaks windows. Large hailstones can injure and sometimes kill small animals.

Because of crop damage, there have been many interesting experiments to suppress hail. Back in the 16th century, farmers used to shoot cannons at thunderstorms thinking this would destroy the hail. Cloud seeding (attempts to start rainfall by distributing dry ice crystals or silver iodide smoke through clouds) is the more modern method, but it is expensive and it is difficult to know how well the method works.

huge amount of damage. They can tear roofs off houses or even blow them over. Mobile homes can be flattened by strong winds in severe thunderstorms. If the ground is dry, the strong wind ahead of a severe thunderstorm causes a dust storm.

Severe thunderstorms bring such chaotic winds near the ground that it is dangerous for airplanes. Weathermen call these chaotic winds microbursts or *wind shear*. These strong ground winds are caused by a strong downdraft which forms inside the severe thunderstorm. When this downdraft hits the ground, it spreads out. Microbursts have caused airplanes to crash while landing or taking off from airports. Many airports have installed instruments to detect the microbursts, so they can warn the pilots.

Tornadoes

S ome thunderstorms give birth to tornadoes. A tornado is a violently rotating, tall, narrow column of wind that makes contact with the ground. The tornado has to touch the ground before it is officially called a tornado. A whirling cloud that does not touch the ground is called a funnel cloud.

Some people confuse hurricanes with tornadoes. Tornadoes are small, while hurricanes cover hundreds of miles or kilometers. However, tornadoes will sometimes form on the edge of hurricanes.

Scientists do not completely understand how tornadoes form. They do know that they often form inside severe thunderstorms that have golf ball-size hail or larger. Tornadoes sometimes occur in a type of severe thunderstorm called a supercell. These supercells are well-organized, long-lasting thunderstorms with warm moist air spiraling upwards. They are generated in much the same way as severe thunderstorms, except they need a few added conditions. Atmospheric scientists have discovered that for tornadoes the updraft needs to be halted for a while, by a layer of warm air just above the ground. As a result, energy inside the storm builds up. Once the updraft is released it explodes upward, like a bullet fired from a gun. Usually, the layer of warm air is overcome when the ground becomes warm enough from sunshine. That is why most tornadoes occur in the afternoon.

Weak tornado near Hodges, Texas.

Most people run from tornadoes, but some scientists run toward them. These people are professional storm chasers. They try to get as close to the tornado as they can. They want to film them and learn more about them. This is not something you should try yourself unless you have a death wish. Some tornado chasers have been struck by lightning, bashed by large hailstones, sucked inside tornadoes, and killed. Storm chasers have learned that a tornado forms in a special spot under the thunderstorm where there is little rain or lightning, in the southwest part of the storm cloud. A tornado usually is found between the strong updraft and

Mobile home destroyed by a tornado.

the downdraft. All strong tornadoes form in a low overhanging cloud that lies just below the thunderstorm. This is called a wall cloud. The spiral inside the thunderstorm is caused by a low-level south or southeast wind being pushed upward. This wind meets with a stronger upper wind that comes from the west or southwest. They cross each other's paths, causing a spin.

Scientists do not understand what causes the 2- to 6-mile-wide (3-10 km) spiral to become narrow and drop out of the sky. The narrowing is similar to the way an ice skater spins. If she pulls her arms in, she spins faster. Still, there is no explanation as to what causes a tornado to descend out of the cloud to the ground. That is why scientists still chase tornadoes — to answer such questions.

Tornadoes vary in size and strength. Some look like thin ropes. These are about a hundred feet across and spin at about 150 mph (240 kph). These are not considered very strong. They touch down only a couple of minutes and then go back up into the cloud. This type of tornado moves at about 25 mph (40 kph). The damage path is only about 150 feet (50 meters) wide and 1 mile (1/2 km) long.

The most dangerous tornadoes are the thick black spiraling clouds that may be 2,000 feet (700 meters) across. These spin at 250 to 300 mph (400 to 480 kph). They sweep across the land at about 50 mph (80 kph). Strong tornadoes can move along the ground for 100 miles (160 km) and have a damage path of over a mile (1.6 km) wide.

Tornadoes are generally unpredictable. They often change shape as they move. They can lift off the ground, go back up into the cloud, and touch down again a short distance away. Just because a tornado has gone back up into a cloud does not mean the danger is over. It can return from the same thunderstorm, or a new tornado can come from a nearby thunderstorm.

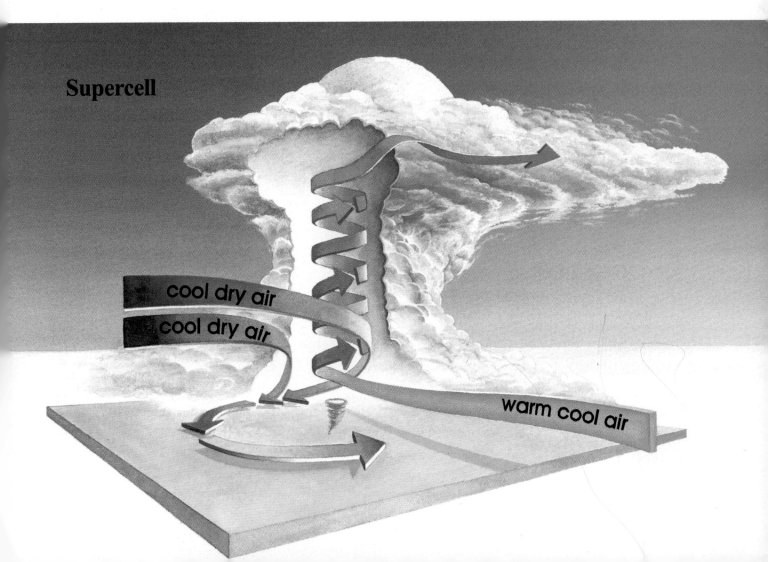

Supercell

cool dry air

cool dry air

warm cool air

Tornado forecasting is the ultimate challenge for a weather forecaster. A tornado *watch* is issued for large areas when atmospheric conditions seem right for tornadoes, but none have occurred yet. A tornado *warning* is issued when a tornado or funnel cloud is sighted or seen on radar. Funnel clouds often drop to the ground and become tornadoes.

A special type of radar, called Doppler radar, is used in weather offices across the United States.

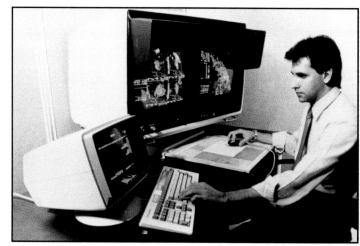

Doppler radar.

They have the unique ability to detect wind speed and direction inside a dangerous thunderstorm. With the new radar, weathermen can see whirling inside the cloud up to 20 minutes before a tornado touches the ground. This radar is especially helpful in *tornado alley* because it gives people enough time to find a safe place. If a big tornado is close to the Doppler radar, it can show up on the screen.

Sometimes, a tornado is difficult to see. All that is visible is the top of the tornado and a small whirl of dust at the ground. These nearly invisible tornadoes fool many people. If you know what to look for, it won't trick you. A concentrated swirl of dust or debris near the ground gives it away. The tornado itself is invisible because water vapor inside the funnel has not yet condensed to form a cloud. Another reason is that not enough dirt and dust have been sucked up into the tornado to mark it.

Most people have heard of the terrible damage that tornadoes cause. Toppled buildings, rolled mobile homes, and uprooted trees are common due to the strong rotating winds. Sometimes they pick up debris that becomes deadly missiles. Tornadoes have even been known to drive a piece of straw into a wood beam. In 1975 a tornado in Mississippi picked up a home freezer and dropped it more than a

How Tornadoes Form

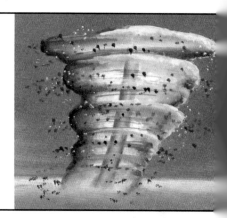

The difference in the wind speed or direction between the ground and the atmosphere about 6,000 feet (1,830 m) off the ground causes eddies (circular spinning of air).

As an eddy moves toward the center of the storm, the updraft sucks it upward. The eddy it tilted upward and stretched.

The eddy becomes vertical. Out of this eddy, the tornado develops below the cloud. The tornado is smaller than the eddy. Scientists are still trying to find out why a gently circulating eddy produces a rapidly spinning tornado.

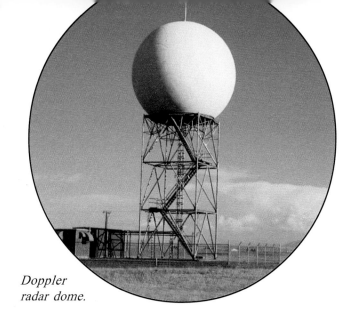

Doppler radar dome.

mile away. Tornadoes passing over barnyards have even stripped chickens of their feathers.

One of the worst tornadoes occurred on April 26, 1989, 40 miles (60 km) north of Dhaka, Bangladesh. A night-time tornado killed 1,109 people, injured 15,000, and left another 100,000 homeless.

The deadliest tornado recorded in the United States was the Tri-State Tornado on March 18, 1925. It developed in southeast Missouri, raced 60 mph (95 kph) through southern Illinois, and broke up in southeast Indiana in about 3 hours and 40 minutes. The city of De Sota, Illinois, was completely destroyed. The tornado killed 689 people, injured 2,000, and left 11,000 homeless.

Sometimes, the atmosphere is especially ripe for a large number of tornadoes in a small area. These are called tornado outbreaks. The worst one in the United States happened on April 3 and 4, 1974. An amazing 148 tornadoes in just two days hit in a 13-state area of the Midwest! The cities of Xenia, Ohio, and Brandenburg, Kentucky, were almost completely destroyed. This outbreak killed

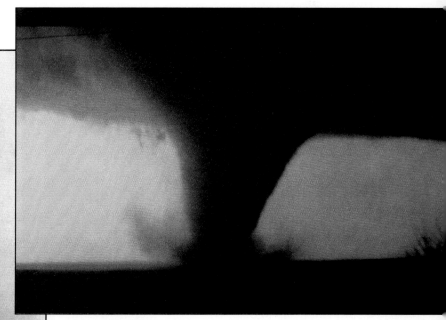

Tornado Classifications

Tornadoes are classified in three ways: weak (69 percent of tornadoes), strong (29 percent of tornadoes), and violent (2 percent of tornadoes, but results in 70 percent of all tornado deaths).

Left — Dissipating tornado near Union City, Oklahoma.
Above — 1979 tornado near Beymour, Texas.

45

Young County, Texas, tornado in May 1994.

that it sounds like 1,000 freight trains roaring down on them. Despite the destruction caused by tornadoes in the United States, only an average of 80 people a year are killed and 1,500 injured. Property damage is usually in the hundreds of millions of dollars. Although the United States' population has increased, the number of tornado deaths has gone down over the years. This is due to improved discovery and warning methods by the National Weather Service. It is expected more lives will be saved as warnings improve.

Dust devils are not tornadoes. You'll see dust devils spiraling upward from a dry field on a hot day. They normally occur under sunny skies and slowly spin between 15 and 30 mph (30 to 50 kph). They are caused by superheated ground resulting in spiralling updrafts.

315 people, injured more than 6,000, and demolished over 9,600 homes.

Although tornadoes occur in many parts of the world, the worst ones are mainly in the southern and central midwest of the United States in the months of April, May, June. This area is called "tornado alley." About 800 tornadoes occur each year in the United States. Only one-third are strong enough to do much damage.

Fortunately, tornadoes are unusual, even in the midwestern United States. Some people live their entire lives in tornado alley and never see one. But if you see one heading for you, it can be very frightening. People who have been in or near a tornado report

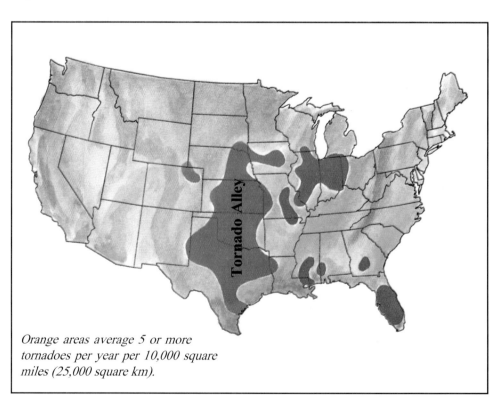

Orange areas average 5 or more tornadoes per year per 10,000 square miles (25,000 square km).

When a tornado touches down on water it is called a waterspout. Although waterspouts are normally weak, one can become stronger if it moves over land. A strong waterspout can sink a small boat. Waterspouts are most frequent in the Atlantic and Indian Oceans near the equator, in the Mediterranean Sea, and in the Gulf of Mexico. Research has shown that the largest number of waterspouts occur in the Florida Keys.

Water spout.

Dust devil.

Safety Tips

Tornado Safety Rules (most also apply for severe thunderstorms)

- Go to the basement or the lowest floor of a house or building. Huddle close to the center of the house or building. Stay away from windows. Find a piece of strong furniture or a mattress to duck under or hide in a closet and wait until it is over.

- If you are in school when a tornado hits, an interior hallway on the lowest floor is safer than a classroom that has windows. Crouch near the wall. Bend over, placing your hands on the back of your head. By all means, stay out of auditoriums, gymnasiums, and other similar structures that have high ceilings.

- Get out of a mobile home; seek shelter elsewhere.

- If caught in a car, get out and seek shelter elsewhere.

- If you cannot find shelter, lie in a ditch or find the lowest, protected ground and cover your head with your hands.

Chapter 6
Hurricanes

Most people think of the tropics as mostly sunny and hot. The tropics is the area of the earth from 30° above to 30° below the equator. The tropical zone looks like a belt wrapped around the stomach of the world. However, large sections of the tropics are rainy and

mild most of the year. These areas are within the Intertropical Convergence Zone (ITCZ), an area where winds from different directions merge (see page 9). The air is forced upward forming many showers and thundershowers. The ITCZ is near the equator. It waters central Africa and the rain forests of Brazil.

Other large sections of the tropics receive drenching rains for six months and are dry for the next six months. The six months of rain is called a monsoon. It is caused by the seasonal changes over the continents. Many tropical areas have

monsoon climates, but India is the most well-known. As Asia cools in winter, cool dry air flows down the Himalaya Mountains, over India, and out into the Indian Ocean. The air is dry because it comes from the continent and sinks down the mountains. During the summer, Asia becomes very warm and the air flow reverses. This causes air from the Indian Ocean to move northward into India and up the Himalaya Mountains. Since this air comes from the warm Indian Ocean, it is very moist. Moving over land the air is forced to rise, forming torrential rain. This rain lasts while Asia is warm. Monsoons usually come with lots of flooding, but since they occur every year, the people are normally prepared.

Three types of storms occur in the tropics. The first is the tropical depression, which is a rainstorm with winds of 38 mph (60 kph) or less. The second is a tropical storm, which has heavy rain and winds between 39 and 74 mph (60 to 120 kph). The third and strongest storm found in the tropics is the hurricane. It has very heavy rain and winds of 75 mph (120 kph) or greater.

Since hurricanes are so destructive, weathermen from all over the world have studied them. They hope their work will help to save lives by giving early warnings. Some people who study hurricanes are called hurricane hunters — pilots who fly into the storm and track it. As they fly into a hurricane, they drop special parachute-borne weather sensors into the storm. These sensors measure the storm characteristics beneath the plane. Messages from the sensor are sent back to the plane. This is very important information because it provides a detailed look at the storm's structure.

Researchers have learned that most hurricanes form after the ocean water warms up past 80°F (27°C). That's why hurricanes north of the equator occur between June and November. Warm water evaporates more quickly than cold water, so

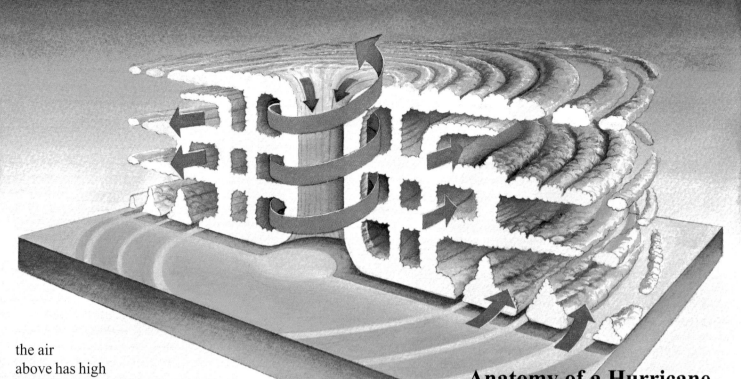

Anatomy of a Hurricane

the air
above has high
amounts of water vapor.
As you recall, water vapor
that condenses to form cloud
droplets gives off heat into the air. This
heat is added to the tropical air that is already
warm. This causes a large pulse of heat to rise
high into the atmosphere. If the winds at the
surface and high in the atmosphere travel in the
same direction, it causes the warm air to concentrate in one spot. The combination of heat and
moisture forms bands of spiraling thunderstorms.
As they spin they blow inward toward the center.
The rain is very heavy in these bands. Between
bands it is either raining lightly or not at all. The
most violent band with the heaviest rain is the

eyewall,
which surrounds
the eye or center of the hurricane. The eye is
normally about 15 miles (24 km) in diameter. All
the updrafts caused by the thunderstorms spread
out when they hit the stratosphere to form a nearly
continuous cloud shield above the storm.

By this time the barometric pressure in the
middle of the mass has dropped, causing the wind
to increase. Wind from the thunderstorms whips
the ocean water into a spray. This, in
turn, increases evaporation from the
ocean, adding more water vapor into
the air, which adds more heat as it
condenses. This results in the air
pressure dropping even more, making
the winds blow even harder. Within a
few days the heat, moisture, pressure,
and wind whip each other into a full-
blown hurricane.

When a hurricane moves inland or
over colder water, it quickly weakens
and falls apart. It loses contact with

Dadeland Mobile Home Park following Hurricane Andrew.

what started and fed the whole process — warm ocean water. Torrential rains, however, may continue even after the wind slows. The reason some hurricanes survive as far north as New England is because a warm ocean current, called the Gulf Stream, continues to provide energy to the storm.

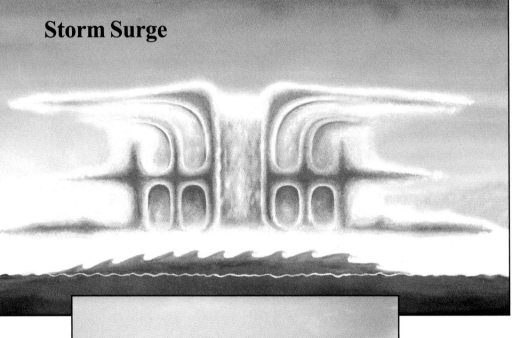

Storm Surge

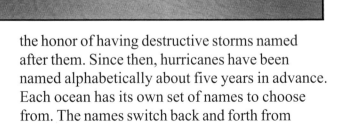

Above — Before Hurricane Andrew; a normal tide at Sewell Park at the mouth of the Miami River.
Right — Water level is still elevated after Andrew passes through.

Generally, six hurricanes a year form in the North Atlantic tropical zone. These storms are pushed by upper winds at about 15-20 mph (24-32 kph) toward the west. Only about two of these storms travel as far north as the east coast of the United States. The other four hurricanes are pushed into the Caribbean Sea or into the Gulf of Mexico. Once in a great while, a storm curves as far north as New England. Fortunately, by the time it gets that far it has lost some of its energy.

Hurricanes occur in other parts of the tropics. However, different names are used for the storms by other countries. In Japan and the Philippines, hurricanes are called typhoons. In the Indian Ocean they are called tropical cyclones. Australians call them willy-willies.

For several hundred years, many hurricanes in the Caribbean were named after a particular saint on whose feast day the hurricane struck. For example, the hurricane that hit Puerto Rico on July 26, 1825, was named "Hurricane Santa Ana." Before the turn of the 20th century, an Australian weatherman named tropical storms after women. This idea caught on, and pretty soon most of the world was giving hurricanes womens' names. This practice came to an end in the United States in 1979. Maybe the women decided that men should share the honor of having destructive storms named after them. Since then, hurricanes have been named alphabetically about five years in advance. Each ocean has its own set of names to choose from. The names switch back and forth from

50

women to men. The naming does not begin until the storm has reached the tropical storm stage.

Hurricanes are the most destructive storms on earth. A hurricane is over 500 miles wide and sets in motion about a million cubic miles of atmosphere. They generate an enormous amount of energy. If we could change the energy of just one hurricane into electricity, the United States would have enough electric power to last three years!

In a hurricane the wind can gust over 200 mph (320 kph). However, it isn't the wind that causes the most deaths in a hurricane. Rather, it's the rising ocean water rushing onto the land that accounts for 90 percent of the deaths. Extremely low air pressure (barometric pressure) inside some hurricanes causes the sea to rise one to three feet above normal. Normal sea level pressure is around 30.00 in. (76 cm). The lowest reading on many barometers is 28.00 in. (71 cm). In many hurricanes, the barometer needle moves way off the end of the scale. The lowest sea level pressure ever recorded on earth was 25.69 in. (65 cm) in Typhoon Tip on October 12, 1979. The low pressure acts like a big vacuum cleaner sucking up the water. As the water rises, strong winds whip it into huge waves, sometimes 50 to 60 feet high (15 to 18 m). The winds are so strong they cause the water to heap up against the shore and pour over the land. This is called a storm surge. These surges can be 15 to 25 feet (5 to 8 m) higher than the normal ocean level. As the water spreads inland, the few people who refuse to leave their homes for higher ground often drown.

Storm surges severely erode beaches, destroy coastal highways, and damage marinas where ships and pleasure boats are tied up. Salt water, when it moves inland, can contaminate lakes and wells. The salt water is poison for animals and people. After Hurricane Andrew struck, snakes crazy from salt poisoning slithered frantically out of Louisiana's flooded bayous and onto roads.

Tornadoes and severe thunderstorms usually happen after the hurricane moves onshore. These storms occur mostly around the hurricane's edge.

The worst hurricane in this century occurred in the Indian Ocean. On November 12, 1970, a hurricane moved north into Bangladesh. On that stormy day a 25-foot (8 m) wall of water struck its shore. Since Bangladesh is very flat, the water rushed over the land, burying everything in its way. The country was devastated, as 300,000 to 500,000 people died. Most of the remaining population were left homeless. Since the country is so poor, there was no communication system in place to warn them. They had no place to go even if they were warned, since there are no mountains in Bangladesh. After the storm, many countries came to their aid. Bangladesh is especially vulnerable to disastrous hurricanes because it is in the tropics, near an ocean, and on flat land. Another less-damaging hurricane struck the country in 1991, killing around 138,000 people. Once again, the world came to its aid.

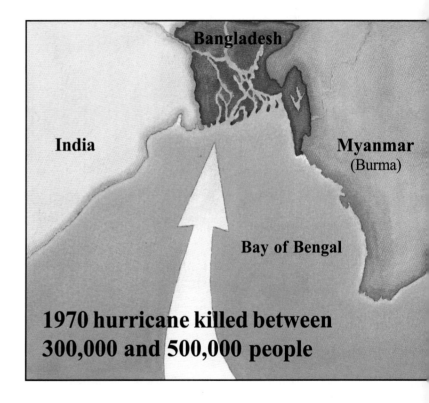

1970 hurricane killed between 300,000 and 500,000 people

In 1900, Galveston, Texas, experienced the deadliest natural disaster in United States history. Galveston is an important U.S. port, located on a long, thin island of sand two miles off the Texas coast. Late that summer a hurricane hit Galveston without warning. A huge wall of water flooded the city within minutes. Most of the city was

Fortunately, hurricanes with the destructive force of Andrew do not happen often.

destroyed; 7,200 people died. Shortly after the storm the people decided to fight back. They worked night and day to raise the level of the land. They hauled tons of dirt onto their island. Then they built cement bulwarks on the Gulf side of the island. So far, these efforts have protected the city from the ocean surges that come with hurricanes.

The year 1992 was a bad one for hurricanes in the United States. Hurricane Iniki developed in the Pacific Ocean off the Central American coast. It curved northwestward and battered Hawaii, inflicting about $2 billion in damage.

Hurricane Andrew struck southern Florida on August 24, 1992. Winds on the ground were reported at 145 mph (232 kph) and gusting to 175 mph (280 kph). It moved west before turning north into Louisiana. The most costly storm in United States history, it wrecked 60,000 homes and left 200,000 people homeless. The damage was estimated at $25 billion. But thanks to an early warning, only 15 people died in Florida and 8 in Louisiana as a direct result of the storm. Hurricane Andrew caused a total of 61 tornadoes and 177 severe storms. Amazingly enough, only 2 people were killed and a few injured by the tornadoes and thunderstorms. Within the next three weeks, another 38 people died from indirect

effects of the hurricane. Many of these people were killed by touching downed electrical wires.

Hurricanes that form in the Pacific Ocean off Central America sometimes strike southern California. Normally, these hurricanes move westward. Most of them run out of energy before they reach halfway across the Pacific Ocean. Once in a great while, upper winds blow a hurricane north to southern California. Even though they aren't as strong when they travel north, they still cause heavy rain and flooding. For example, by the time Hurricane Norman reached southern California in 1978, it was downgraded to a tropical depression. Even so, it caused about $500 million in damage.

For most of U.S. history, hurricanes came without warning. Many ships at sea were surprised by hurricanes and sank. Much treasure from old ships still lies on the ocean bottom, thanks to hurricanes. We can thank God that those days are over. The Galveston and other hurricane disasters prompted the U.S. government to establish a hurricane warning branch. Over the years, hurricane forecasting has greatly improved. In 1943 a hurricane forecast center was established in Miami, Florida. The National Weather Service's National Hurricane Center has since been moved to Coral Gables, Florida. There the latest computer technology and most sophisticated atmospheric weather programs are run on high-speed computers. Their job is to predict a hurricane's size, intensity, movement, and storm surge. The Center issues a hurricane watch if it is believed the hurricane will hit a certain area within 24 to 36 hours. A hurricane warning is issued if the storm is forecast to hit within 24 hours or less.

Satellites, 22,000 miles out in space, can see hurricanes form and watch their movement. Hurricanes are easy to recognize. They look like giant cloud doughnuts or pinwheels. They can now be detected long before they reach the U.S. coastline. Satellite information also is used as input into the computer models. When a hurricane draws near, many coastal Doppler weather radars track the storm's details.

Since the 1920s, the average amount of deaths in the United States has decreased. The saving of lives was due not only to better hurricane forecasts, but also because of hurricane preparedness efforts. People at all levels of emergency services spend years educating people, planning evacuation routes, and building special shelters. Before Andrew struck, 2 million people were evacuated to safety in Florida and Louisiana.

Although many lives are being saved, property damage has increased greatly since the 1920s. Hurricane Andrew alone caused $25 billion in

Black Point Marina after Hurricane Andrew's wind and storm surge picked up and tossed the boats like toys.

damage. This is partly due to more people living in hurricane-prone areas. One problem is that many people have built homes in very vulnerable locations. Millions live next to the beach. Some have built on low barrier islands offshore. Fortunately, hurricanes are rather rare; the very strong ones, like Andrew, even more rare. The worse part of the hurricane, the eye, impacts only a small part of the coast. As more people build in vulnerable areas, a greater chance exists that more people will be killed in hurricanes.

Safety Tips

If a watch is issued:
- Turn refrigerator to the coldest setting to preserve food longer.
- Keep your car fueled.
- Have plenty of emergency supplies stored, such as canned food, batteries, propane for camp stoves, extra money, etc.
- Fill water bottles and the bathtub with water.
- Review family evacuation plans.
- Bring pets indoors.
- Bring outdoor objects inside the house or garage.
- Make sure medical supplies are available.

If a warning is issued:
- Board up windows and garage.
- Unplug appliances.
- Be prepared to evacuate.

Chapter 7
Winter Storms

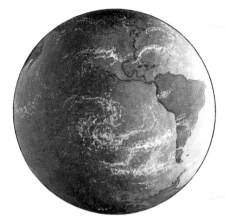

Seasons determine the type of weather during the year. Most areas have four seasons. In the previous chapters we have discussed warm weather storms, but winter storms are very different.

The seasons are caused by the earth's tilt on its axis as it orbits around the sun. The earth's axis is an imaginary line that goes from the North Pole to the South Pole. The earth rotates once every 24 hours on this axis, which tilts at a 23.5 degree angle. The tilt causes daylight hours to grow shorter as winter approaches.

In the winter, less sunshine during short days and long nights causes cooler temperatures. The shortest day of the year in the Northern Hemisphere is at the end of December. In the far north, near the North Pole, there is no sunshine during much of the winter, so the polar areas become very cold.

As the earth continues its yearly course around the sun, winter changes to summer and the days soon become longer. Long days give the sun more time to warm the ground and atmosphere. The long days of sunshine give us summer warmth. The tropics either have no seasons or very small changes in temperature; so they stay warm most of the time. However, a seasonal change in precipitation, called the monsoon, causes some tropical areas to be very rainy at times.

Thunderstorms occur less during autumn. In the Northern Hemisphere the hurricane season ends around December 1. As temperatures drop, rain and snowstorms are more frequent, usually lasting a day or two and bringing large amounts of moisture. Geography decides which it will be. Snow usually falls in the northern section of North America, Europe, and Asia. Rain generally falls further south, closer to the equator. The west coasts of the United States, Canada, and Europe rarely experience snow. Relatively warm winds from the ocean blow onto the land keeping

Spring.

Summer.

Fall.

Winter.

it too warm for snow. Although Ireland is far north, the warm Gulf Stream current causes mild winters with little snow.

The climate on North America's east coast differs from the west coast. This is because the prevailing west wind on the east coast blows from off the snowy continent bringing the cold, wintery air with it. The warm Atlantic Ocean doesn't modify this situation much because the winds usually blow from the wrong direction.

Snow is a wonderful creation by God; it is not only beautiful but useful. It gently floats from the sky, each delicate flake having its own crystalline shape. The snow creates a fluffy, protective blanket for plants, seeds, and tiny animals, shielding them from the harsh winter. It is fun to play in and sled down hills.

High in the mountains, storm after storm piles the snow deeper and deeper. This snowpack becomes nature's water preserve. In the spring it will gradually melt and replenish the rivers, streams, reservoirs, and ground water.

Have you ever wondered why God made snow white? He did it for a special reason. When sunlight glistens on the snow, most of its rays are reflected into space. This allows the snow to melt slowly. The meltwater then percolates deep into the soil. This gradual melting makes flooding minimal.

The universe enjoys harmony and beauty, but once in a while a wild storm here or there shows that all is not perfect. Our world has been contaminated with sin; because of that not everything works as God originally planned. Just as some summer storms become dangerous, so also do some winter storms. It is wise to know how to protect ourselves from these events.

Most winter rainstorms in the southern United States are a blessing. The rain soaks deep into the ground to be used the next spring for growing crops. Winter rains add water to streams, rivers, springs, and wells. However, in California heavy rain storms cause problems. For example, because southern California is so far south, its winter air is warm. Warmer air can hold more water vapor. Southern California is also next to the ocean,

close to the vapor source. So its winter rains are especially heavy. Rain pours even harder on the mountains and hills around Los Angeles. After the normally dry land becomes soaked, little streams of water course their way down the hillsides and erode the soil on the way. In the worst conditions these streams cause mudslides to sweep down the hills. The problem becomes especially serious after a forest or brush fire destroys the soil-stabilizing vegetation. Many people have built houses on these hillsides. Sometimes after heavy rains, the soil and their homes slide down the hill.

Snowstorms are exciting and beautiful, but if a person does not know their dangers they can be injured or die. When a winter storm begins, it is wiser to watch it from your window than to be outside. Snow in a storm falls very fast and is often whipped into large drifts. A snowstorm is called a blizzard when the winds are over 35 mph (56 kph) and you can't see ahead because of blowing and falling snow.

Winter storms and blizzards can deposit several feet of snow that blow into huge drifts. Sometimes the drifts are over ten feet tall. They can even cover a house. Winter storms can completely paralyze a city; stranding people at airports, stopping the flow of supplies, and disrupting emergency services. They can cause power poles and trees to topple. Extremely heavy snow can even cave in a roof. People who live in rural

areas, especially, may be isolated for days. Cows and sheep can become stranded and die of the cold. In the mountains, heavy snow sometimes leads to avalanches. The arctic cold that comes behind a winter storm can cause ice jams on rivers and streams.

Many famous winter storms are part of North America's history. In 1846 the Donner Party journeyed by covered wagon from Illinois headed for Sutter's Fort near Sacramento, California. As a result of bad decisions and slow going, they tried to cross the high Sierra Nevada Mountains in late October. Usually, California is still fairly warm at that time of year. As the party surveyed the Sierra Nevada Mountains, they did not see any snow. However, shortly after they left, huge snowstorms

hit the mountains. They were forced to camp near Truckee, California. The snow was so deep their wagon wheels became stuck. It was very cold. They tried to wait the storm out, but when one storm ended, another began. Their supplies dwindled. Some of the party decided to hike out and find help rather than starve. Most of them died in the attempt. Many of those who stayed behind lived. Of the 87 people who started in Illinois only 47 survived.

On March 12–15, 1993, a winter storm now called the "Storm of the Century" struck eastern North America. A huge blizzard developed in the northern Gulf of Mexico then curved northeast up the east coast. Fortunately for the East, this kind of storm hits only once in a hundred years. The last storm of this size hit the northeastern United States in 1888. The 1993 storm was a powerful Northeaster — a storm which moves northeast along the east coast. The winds ahead of the storm are from the northeast and pick up large amounts of water vapor from the warm Gulf Stream Current. All this water vapor ends up as heavy rain close to the ocean and deep snow inland.

The Storm of the Century affected the entire east coast. It caused 15 tornadoes and severe

How Temperature Affects Winter Precipitation

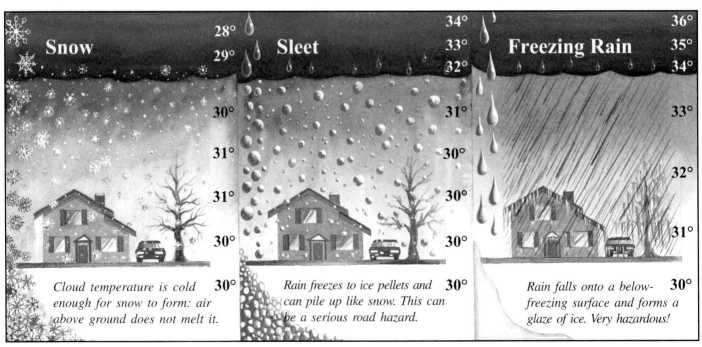

Snow 28° 29° 30° 31° 31° 30° 30°
Cloud temperature is cold enough for snow to form: air above ground does not melt it.

Sleet 34° 33° 32° 31° 30° 30° 30°
Rain freezes to ice pellets and can pile up like snow. This can be a serious road hazard.

Freezing Rain 36° 35° 34° 33° 32° 31° 30°
Rain falls onto a below-freezing surface and forms a glaze of ice. Very hazardous!

thunderstorms in Florida which killed 44 people. The wind and low pressure caused a 12-foot-high storm surge to hit the east coast. Six inches (15 cm) of snow fell on the Florida panhandle in March, which is unusual.

As the storm ripped northeast up the east coast, heavy wet snow was driven by strong

hurricane force winds. The winds piled the snow into huge drifts. When the snow stopped, it totaled 56 in. (142 cm) deep in Mount LeConte, Tennessee. It was 50 in. (127 cm) on Mount Mitchell, North Carolina; 44 in. (112 cm) in Snowshoe, West Virginia; 43 in. (109 cm) at Syracuse, New York; 36 in. (91 cm) at Latrobe, Pennsylvania; 35 in. (89 cm) at Lincoln, New Hampshire; 29 in. (74 cm) in Page County, Virginia; 24 in. (61 cm) in Mountain city, Georgia; 19 in. (48 cm) at Portland, Maine; and 17 in. (43 cm) near Birmingham, Alabama. The storm obviously affected a very large area.

The highest winds gusted to 131 mph (210 kph) at Grand Etang, Nova Scotia. In many other areas from Florida to southeast Canada the winds gusted to over 70 mph (112 kph). Hundreds of roofs collapsed, thousands of people were stranded, and millions were without electricity. For the first time in U.S. history, every major airport on the east coast was closed at one time or

another because of the storm. Interstate highways from Atlanta northward were closed, two ships sank, and the pounding surf destroyed houses along the coast. At least 270 people were killed and 48 were missing at sea — three times the combined death toll from Hurricanes Andrew and Hugo. Property damage was estimated at $5 billion. It was the country's costliest winter storm ever.

Also dangerous are ice storms, caused by rain falling into a lower atmosphere that is below freezing. This temperature condition near the ground is called an inversion. The air above is warmer than the air close to the ground. When raindrops fall into the lower layer of below-freezing air, they become supercooled but not frozen. Supercooled drops freeze when they are jostled. Sometimes the

raindrops freeze before they hit the ground. These are called ice pellets or sleet. Ice pellets are not nearly as dangerous as freezing rain. When drops of liquid rain freeze on objects, a shimmering layer of ice coats everything. Cities are transformed into crystal palaces. Icicles drip from trees and telephone wires. Ice covers roads and cars. The ice glimmers and sparkles in the sun. It is beautiful, but nearly impossible to drive or walk on. Walking on sidewalks of ice becomes a slippery adventure. Once in awhile, telephone or

electrical wires snap from the weight of the ice. After a freezing rainstorm, avoid broken electrical lines.

Winter storms are caused a by strong temperature difference between the tropics and the mid and high latitudes. The mid latitudes range from approximately 35° to 60° latitude. In the Northern Hemisphere the high latitudes extend from 60° latitude to the North Pole. As winter approaches the earth cools in the mid and high latitudes. The cooling creates a large temperature difference between the tropics and the poles. For instance, the change in temperature from Texas to northern Saskatchewan, Canada, can vary 100°F (56°C). When strong temperature differences are concentrated in a small area, they create a front. Winter storms tend to develop along the front. The jet steam is usually above the front to steer the storm, usually from west to east.

The U.S. National Weather Service issues watches and warnings for winter storms, blizzards, and ice storms. They also issue advisories for such things as blowing snow, high winds, dense fog, etc. Many other countries do the same. A winter storm watch is posted if a storm may come within 12 to 48 hours. The weatherperson is not sure the storm will develop but the watch is issued if a good possibility exists of a storm moving into the area. When the storm is nearly certain or is occurring, the watch is upgraded to a winter storm warning.

Winter storms can be dangerous for a number of reasons. Frostbite and hypothermia can occur. When a severe wind chill factor is in operation, a person's exposed skin can freeze. When a person has frostbite, their skin becomes pale and numb. The most susceptible parts of the body are fingers, toes, ear lobes, and the tip of the nose. Hypothermia happens when a person is out in the cold so long that the body temperature drops below normal. He or she starts shivering and is unable to stop. The person then becomes confused and forgets where they are. Speech becomes slurred and the words don't make sense. Soon he or she becomes very tired and wants to sleep, anywhere. If someone gets hypothermia,

Winter storms are considered deceptive killers because most deaths are indirectly related to the storm. For example, 70 percent of all winter deaths are the result of accidents involving people driving on icy and

wrap the victim in blankets and take him or her to the hospital emergency ward. If it's impossible to get to a hospital quickly, do all you can to gradually warm the individual.

dangerous roads. Another 25 percent of storm-related deaths happen to people caught outside in storms with no shelter available. The core body temperature falls, and the victim dies of hypothermia. Most of that 25 percent who die are men over 40 years old. Some people die of heart attacks while shoveling snow.

Safety Tips

- Make sure you have enough stored food, and batteries for a radio and flashlight in either your house or car.
- Avoid unnecessary travel.
- If you must go outside, dress with several layers of warm clothes. Do not overexert yourself, such as shoveling snow, pushing a car, or walking in deep snow. Sweating could lead to a chill and hypothermia. Find shelter. Cover all of the exposed parts of your body, and try to keep dry. Wait calmly for the storm to end; they usually don't last too long without a break.
- If you must drive, carry sleeping bags for every person and keep your gas tank full. Let someone know your destination.
- If you get stuck, stay in your vehicle. Remain visible to rescuers by keeping an overhead light on, and attach a bright-colored cloth to your antenna. As you sit in the car, move around to keep warm. You can run the engine and heater for a brief period, but check to be sure the exhaust pipe is not plugged. Also, keep one window slightly cracked to prevent carbon monoxide poisoning.

Chapter 8
Wild Weather

An unusual phenomenon is St. Elmo's Fire. Once in a great while, during a night-time lightning storm, people look toward the mountains and see eerie glows of light outlining sharp mountain peaks. Pilots occasionally report seeing their wing tips aglow. Unseasoned sailors at sea have been frightened when their ship's mast began to glow.

St. Elmo's Fire is caused by a high charge of electricity in the air. It normally occurs when there are thunderstorms in the area. Electricity in the air causes pointed objects to glow faintly. A person who did not know what it was might think some heavenly being was visiting. St. Elmo's fire received its name from Mediterranean sailors who regarded it as a visitation by their patron saint, Erasmus, or Elmo. It was thought to be a good omen by the superstitious sailors because it tends to occur in the last phases of a violent thunderstorm. This is the time when the thunderstorm is decaying and the ocean is calming down. Often sailors have praised God for the reassurance of St. Elmo's fire and been awestruck by its beauty.

When people think of Hawaii, they think of beautiful white sandy beaches and basking in the warm sunshine. But one point in the Hawaiian Islands has the highest yearly rainfall *in the world*. Mount Waialeale, on the northwestern island of Kauai, receives an average 460 in. (1,168 cm) of rain per year. That's almost 40 feet (12 m) of rain annually. Hawaii has unique mountainous geography and plentiful sunshine. The atmosphere around the islands carries a large amount of water vapor. Northeast trade winds gently blow across the tropical ocean picking up huge amounts of water vapor. As the winds move up the mountains on Kauai, the wet air cools and condenses into clouds. As the day becomes warmer, the clouds quickly develop into thunderstorms. Slow upper winds give them plenty of time to generously release their moisture. That's why Mt. Waialeale experiences so much rain.

In Washington state, you can start from a rain forest, travel east over the Cascade Mountains, and enter into a desert — all within several hours. The western slopes of the Olympic Mountains receive so much rain and snow the area is considered to be a rain forest. They collect their abundant rain in the same way as Mt. Waialeale in Hawaii. The rain falls as moisture-laden air climbs the mountains. In Washington

Western Washington's Ho rain forest.

Eastern Washington wheat field.

state, however, the moisture is cool and comes from the northern Pacific Ocean. Many of the mountains collect over 100 in. (254 cm) of water a year. In fact, the greatest snow fall in any one year in North America is 1,122 in. (2,850 cm) at Paradise Ranger Station, located at about 5,000 feet (1,525 m) elevation on Mount Rainier. That's an amazing 93.5 feet of snow.

As you travel over the Cascade Mountains and down the east side, the climate becomes drier. By the time you reach Yakima or Pasco, Washington, it's practically a desert. Yakima receives only 7 in. (18 cm) of rainfall a year. As the west winds continue east and blow down the Cascade Mountains, the air becomes warmer and drier. Just as rising air cools and becomes more moist, the opposite happens when the air sinks to lower altitudes. Washington state's climate dramatically illustrates the difference a mountain range makes on the weather and climate. The windward side (toward the wind) is a rain forest; the leeward side (away from the wind) is nearly a desert.

Foehn Winds

A foehn (pronounced fone) wind is relatively warm and dry, descending down a mountain front. These occur in almost all mountain regions of the mid and high latitudes, most frequently during the colder time of year. Foehn winds are common east of the high Andes Mountains. They are well-known in Japan, New Zealand, and eastern and central Asia. Foehn winds also blow from the Greenland Ice Sheet down to the coast. Even Antarctica experiences foehn winds near some mountains.

The word "foehn" originated from the European Alps. Due to storms moving across northern Europe, south and west winds blow down the north and east slopes of the Alps. Even though the winds generally blow strong, the weather is quite mild. Foehn winds are especially prevalent where north-south valleys open onto the plains or in large east-west valleys. It was at Innsbruck, Austria, where foehn winds were actively studied. Besides warmer, drier air, foehn winds typically come with extraordinarily good visibility. The mountains can appear unusually close. Near the

mountains, a wall of cumulus-like clouds are observed. These clouds are called the foehn wall. Out from the mountains lens-shaped clouds at medium levels in the atmosphere are seen. These are called altocumulus lenticularis.

In the United States, especially along the east slopes of the Rocky Mountains from Alberta, Canada, to New Mexico, foehn winds are called chinooks (pronounced shinooks). Chinook is an Indian word meaning snow eater. These mild, gusty west winds can melt a lot of snow within a few days or less. For long stretches of winter, chinook winds keep the eastern slopes of the Rocky Mountains and the high plains snow-free. Tens of thousands of elk and deer move from their mountain home to spend the winter and find dry grass in these areas.

However, chinook winds occasionally become very strong and dangerous. They can fan grass fires out of control. East Glacier, Montana, and Boulder, Colorado, are well-known for their damaging chinook winds which have peaked up to 125 mph (200 kph). Trucks and campers are blown off the road every year, and even trains have been derailed around East Glacier, where homes are tied down by hurricane straps. In

Foehn wind over Hope Bay, Antarctica.

61

Montana, the temperature rose from -32°F (-36°C) to 15°F (-9°C) in just 7 minutes.

This rapid seesaw in temperature causes unusual moisture effects. When arctic air retreats back up into Canada, the sparse water vapor from the chinook wind condenses as frost on the cold pavement. This is dangerous for drivers because, although the road still looks dry, it's very slippery. Even car windows will quickly frost coming from the cold arctic air into the warm chinook. The cold windshield's contact with the warm chinook air causes rapid condensation of water vapor on the windshield. Suddenly, all the windows turn white. This is dangerous

Santa Ana winds can cause billions of dollars of damage in southern California. Fires often start; some by natural causes and others by arson. The dry winds blowing in great gusts through the mountain valleys can cause firestorms that burn enormous amounts of acreage and homes, and often take armies of firefighters days to put out.

strong winds hanging houseplants sway indoors. A cooperative weather observer from East Glacier used to know when the wind exceeded 90 mph (144 kph), because at that speed an old defective toilet would flush. The National Weather Service issues high wind warnings for potentially damaging chinook winds.

When cold arctic air from Canada meets the chinook winds, it causes some enormous temperature changes. Browning, Montana, dropped 100°F (56°C) in 24 hours in January 1916. The temperature fell from 44°F (7°C) to -56°F (-49°C). In just 27 minutes, Spearfish, South Dakota, fell 58°F (32°C), from 54°F (12°C) to -4°F (-20°C). It can warm up just as fast when a chinook blows into the area. On January 11, 1981, in Great Falls,

because the driver can't see the road.

Another famous foehn wind is called the Santa Ana wind of California. It blows westward from the mountains of southern California to the coast when a high pressure area settles over Nevada, Utah, and Idaho. As the air descends down the mountains, temperatures can rise to 100°F (38°C) in winter by the time they reach the coast. In some canyons the wind can blow over 100 mph (160 kph). This is because of the funnel effect caused by wind flowing through a narrow opening in a mountain range. Sometimes these winds pick up massive amounts of dust. The Santa Ana winds are so dry that fires fan out of control. They can occur at any time of the year.

Great Lakes Weather

In the eastern United States, the sky normally clears after an arctic cold front passes. However, in the Great Lakes area of the United States and Canada, the opposite occurs. Clouds rise as cold and dry arctic air blows over the comparatively warm Great Lakes. The large temperature difference between the arctic air and the lake water causes a high amount of evaporation to occur. The fact that arctic air is very dry enhances its ability to absorb moisture from the lakes. So, when all this water vapor hits the opposite shoreline, it causes heavy snow squalls to form. The faster the wind speed and the longer the wind blows over the water, the heavier the snow. These snowstorms have been known to deposit up to 102 in. (259 cm) of snow in 5 days. The 1976–77 winter was drier than normal in the eastern United States. The colder than normal temperatures, however, caused 467 in. (1,186 cm) of snow to fall at Hooker, New York.

Lake effect snowstorms can occur at many locations around the Great Lakes. The main area of snow is close to the lake, but snow squalls can drop snow up to 100 miles (160 km) downwind from the water. This explains why Buffalo, New York, receives so much snow. Buffalo is located at the eastern end of Lake Erie. Heavy snow at Buffalo occurs when the wind direction is out of the west, blowing the length of Lake Erie.

Ball Lightning

An unusual sight in a thunderstorm is ball lightning — a glowing ball of light. Those who have seen it say it's the size of a grapefruit or basketball; it has even been reported to be as large as a car. The glowing ball is either red, orange, or yellow. A few people have seen it falling from the clouds. On occasion, ball lightning hovers or glides just above the ground for a few seconds, or it can roll on the surface of an object. Hissing noises come from the fiery orb. Some have even mistaken it for a UFO. Ball lightning sometimes explodes loudly, while other times it just quietly fades away. It has been known to pass through an open window, hopping and sizzling across the floor. It can then disappear into electrical outlets, into the television set, or even go up the chimney. Scientists do not understand ball lightning very well. Some scientists question the reality of ball lightning since it is so strange. However, it has been widely reported in weather journals by trustworthy observers. So, it likely is real.

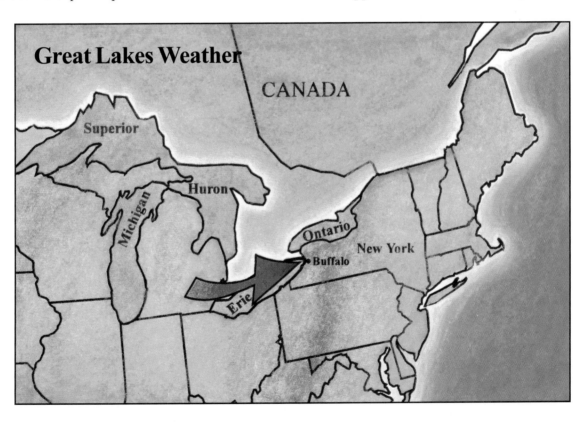

Great Lakes Weather

CANADA

Superior

Huron

Michigan

Ontario

New York

Buffalo

Erie

Chapter 9
Climate in the Past

Scientists have studied the earth's rocks, ice sheets, and ocean sediments for many years. One reason is to learn about the planet's past climate. Scientists hope that by learning about the climate in the prehistoric past they can predict future climatic changes. Over the years, they have made many perplexing discoveries they have trouble explaining.

Scientists have found abundant evidence from rocks and fossils of warm climates in the past. Some of these warm-climate fossils were found at high latitudes, close to the poles. For instance, dinosaur fossils along with warm climate trees and mammals, were discovered in Alaska, northern Canada, and Siberia. Dinosaur fossils were also found in Antarctica!

In northern Canada's Arctic Islands, about 600 miles from the North Pole, scientists have found many fossilized swamp cypress trees. These trees grow today in the warm, humid swamps of Georgia and Florida. They also found fossils of crocodiles, whose descendants mostly live today in tropical locations. The average winter temperature in that cold north region today is -40°F (-40°C).

Hippopotamus fossils have been found in southern England, France, and western Germany. In southern England, reindeer fossils were found close to hippopotamus fossils. Hippopotami normally live in warm regions. Reindeer live in cold regions. These fossils were found in the very top sediment layers associated with the Ice Age.

Crocodiles have been found living in partially dried up lakes in the western Sahara Desert. Scientists have explored the Sahara Desert and found abundant fossils of hippopotami, elephants, giraffes, crocodiles, and other animals. They also found fossils of fish and clams. They even discovered that humans lived in the Sahara with these animals. There are tens of thousands of rock art pictures painted by men. These pictures show many types of animals, people, and even whole villages that once existed in the Sahara Desert.

Scientists have sent radar beams from satellites through the desert sands of the eastern Sahara. The pictures that came back were startling. They show old river channels, some quite large, in an area that now receives rain once every 50 years. So, the Sahara Desert was once lush and well-watered.

Much evidence exists that at one time huge lakes occupied most arid or semiarid areas of the world. Like the Sahara Desert, lakes were abundant in the southwestern United States. The Great Salt Lake in Utah was once 800 feet (244 m) deeper and six times its size. You can see distinct shore-lines high up on the sides of hills and mountains around the lake. Other lakes existed in Nevada, and at one time Death Valley had a lake. Where did all this water come from?

Scientists have found bones from hundreds of thousands of woolly mammoths in Siberia, as well as in Alaska. Villagers also found bones from woolly rhinoceroses, elk, deer, and many other animals in the same area. A few mammoths were frozen with food inside their stomachs and stuck be-tween their teeth. These animals are associated with the Ice Age, since they are often found in river flood sediments. Also, the bones of woolly mam-

moths and other animals are commonly found all over the Northern Hemisphere, near the edge of where the ice sheets used to be.

All these woolly mammoth bones in Siberia are very strange. The farther north, the more bones are found. Bones and tusks were even found on the islands and on the shallow ocean bottom of the Arctic Ocean and the Bering Sea. Woolly mammoths required a huge amount of food and probably moderate weather. Why would they have lived in such a place as Siberia and Alaska where the land is frozen most of the year and food in short supply?

During the summer, the frozen ground in that cold region only melts a few feet down. The pooling water creates massive bogs. It would have been nearly impossible for a large animal to walk in the sticky bogs. They would become stuck and die, if they hadn't died of starvation during the winter first. The climate in Siberia and Alaska had to have been vastly different for these animals to have lived there.

Many warm climate plant and tree fossils have been found in polar regions.

Noah's Flood — Key to the Past

It is important to understand that the study of the past, or prehistory, is not science. This is because the scientific method requires that past processes, such as past climate, be observed. We cannot repeat or observe the past. For example, we can observe the temperature outside at any moment by looking at a thermometer. That is scientific. If we wanted to know the temperature 5,000 years ago, there is no way we can observe this temperature. Any educated guess we make is not scientific. None of the requirements for the scientific method can be fulfilled when a scientist studies the past, whether he believes in evolution or creation.

In order to determine the climate of the past, a scientist must make assumptions about the past. From these assumptions, he develops a model. A model is like a model airplane; it is a representation of the real airplane. A model of the past is a representation of what a scientist thinks happened in the past. Then the scientist looks at data he observes in the present world. He tests how well the observed data in the present fits his model. With models, one studies all evidence of the past including rocks, fossils, the Bible, and other written records.

There are two main models for the prehistoric past. These models are built on different assumptions. One model is called the creation-Genesis flood model. Those who hold to this model believe the Bible gives us accurate history of the past. They believe that God was the only accurate observer at the time. He is powerful enough to have the past history accurately recorded in His Bible. This model believes that God created everything after its own kind and to reproduce after its own kind, and not into some other kind. Those who believe the creation-Genesis flood model also believe most of the sedimentary rocks, the layer-caked rocks seen all over the world, were laid down in Noah's worldwide flood.

The other model is the evolution-uniformitarian model. This model assumes that every organism that has ever lived is a product of millions of years of evolution, and they also believe that the rocks were formed by slow processes of erosion and sedimentation that we observe today. This is where the prefix uniform comes from in uniformitarianism. They believe in uniform or slow processes over millions of years. Uniformitarianism is a good assumption for recent times. However, these scientists extend uniformitarianism to account for all past rocks. This assumption automatically eliminates Noah's flood.

With two different models and beginning assumptions, a scientist can look at the data we observe at present and draw conclusions about that data. Sometimes scientists, looking at the same data, will draw completely different conclusions. This is because they each believe in a different model.

The different assumptions and conclusions of the two models are especially important to understand. They can be illustrated by how each looks at sedimentary rocks. Most rocks on the surface of the earth are sedimentary rocks. All of these rocks were once mud, sand, and pebbles that were carried and deposited by water. With time or pressure these sediments hardened and became sandstone, shale, and conglomerate. The sediments form layers, like the layers of a cake.

A geologist can study river erosion processes for many years. He observes the river and studies its banks, its channel, the amount of sediment (dirt the water carries), erosion, and deposition. He concludes that water in the river gradually eroded or wore away the river's banks. He sees that it deposited the sediment a little downriver along the bank, on a flood plain, or carried the sediment into the ocean. This is scientific because he observes these processes happening in the present. However, he then concludes that repeated erosion and deposition of sediments over millions of years explains all the sedimentary rocks in the world, like the great thickness of hardened sediments seen in the Grand Canyon. Of course, if the sediments seen in the Grand Canyon formed by uniform, present process, it would take millions of years to collect. This is one reason scientists who believe the evolution-uniformitarian model believe in millions and billions of years of past earth history.

Scientists who believe the Bible is God's Word know that about 5,000 years ago the earth experienced a gigantic global flood. The Genesis flood could easily explain how sedimentary rocks were laid down quickly — not by present processes. It was not a little water over millions of years, but a lot of water over a *short* period of time. Assuming Noah's flood took place, evolutionary scientists would be wrong about how the majority of sedimentary rocks were formed. They would also be wrong about how much time it would take to deposit all the sediments, such as the sediments in the Grand Canyon.

Evolutionary scientists would also be mistaken about past climates. Fossils of warm-climate animals and plants in polar regions are very difficult to explain by the evolutionary-uniformitarian model. Take for example, dinosaurs and swamp cypress have been discovered near the poles. Present processes could not explain such findings. The creation-Genesis flood model has several possible explanations for these fossils. There could have been a warm climate in polar regions due to a vapor canopy before the flood, as some creationists believe. A vapor canopy would have kept the earth warm. The high latitude animals and plants could also have been swept poleward from tropical locations by powerful currents during the flood.

The Ice Age

The worldwide flood set the stage for the Ice Age. Due to a much different geography and the effects of the flood, the climate would have been very different for a while after the flood. Volcanoes would have continued erupting. Volcanic ash and gases would have reflected much of the warm sunshine back to space, cooling the ground. Summers would have been much colder over the land.

Enormous amounts of water vapor rose from the warm ocean and blew onto the cool continents. Snow fell in the northern latitudes year around. Snow piled up as storm after storm blew onto the continents. Eventually the sheer weight of the snow compacted into ice. Soon, ice sheets developed over northern North America, northern Europe, and northwest Asia. Greenland and Antarctica developed ice sheets that we can still see today.

With time, volcanic eruptions slowed down and the ocean temperature became cooler. More sunlight reached the ground. Less water evaporated from cooler oceans. So the Ice Age quickly ended. It only lasted about 700 years. There was only one Ice Age because there was only one flood that changed the climate. There also will never be another ice age. (For more information, see the author's children's book: *Life in the Great Ice Age*.)

Scientists who believe in the evolution-uniformitarian model have difficulty accounting for the Ice Age. It is extremely difficult for ice sheets to form in the present climate. That is why more than 60 theories have been invented to try to account for the Ice Age. All these theories have serious difficulties.

The Ice Age caused by the Genesis flood can explain many of the perplexing mysteries of the past. The evolution-uniformitarian model has great difficulty explaining these mysteries. Consider the hippopotamus fossils found in western

Maximum extent of Ice Age.

The oceans would have been very warm after the flood. Hot water would have been added to the pre-flood ocean from the "fountains of the great deep." Volcanoes, lava flows, and earth movements would have added more heat. The ocean water would have been warm all the way to the poles. The Arctic Ocean could have had a temperature of 80°F (27°C) for a while.

Mount St. Helens, July 22, 1980, eruption.

Europe. During the beginning of the Ice Age, hippopotami would be able to migrate to southern England because of the proximity to the warm ocean water. The warm Atlantic Ocean would bathe western Europe in warm air. Eventually, as the climate turned colder, the hippos would die and end up fossilized along with reindeer, musk oxen, and woolly mammoths in Ice Age deposits.

Storm tracks would have been different during the post-flood Ice Age. One storm track likely reached down into the Sahara Desert, bringing milder, wet weather. The Sahara would have bloomed with animals and people after the flood. Unfortunately, at the end of the Ice Age the weather patterns changed to what they are now. The Sahara gradually became a desert. The animals either migrated or died of starvation or thirst. A few crocodiles were able to survive in partially dried up lakes into the 19th or 20th century. These crocodiles show that the change in the Sahara Desert occurred not that long ago.

Both the Genesis flood and the Ice Age can explain the abundant evidence of lakes and rivers that once existed in areas that are now desert. The initial filling of the lakes is easily explained by the flood. When the flood waters receded, basins that had no outlets would remain filled with water. During the Ice Age the much wetter climate would maintain the lakes with streams and rivers for at least several hundred years. After the Ice Age, the lakes would mostly dry up. The evolution-uniformitarian model has serious difficulty filling up these lakes in a cool, dry Ice Age climate. Their model requires at least six times more water flowing into the Great Salt Lake for the water level to rise 800 feet (244 m).

As you may have realized, the creation-Genesis flood model can explain the woolly mammoths in Siberia by the unique Ice Age climate after the flood. A warm Arctic and North Pacific Ocean would have kept Siberia, as well as Alaska, comfortable during winter. As a result these areas would have no permafrost and no massive summer bogs. The moisture from the warm oceans would have kept these areas well-watered. Vegetation would be lush, so the animals would have had plenty to eat. But towards the end of the Ice Age, the oceans would cool and the climate of Siberia would become colder and drier. The Arctic Ocean would have quickly frozen. One day during late summer or early autumn, a particularly cold snowstorm devastated many of the woolly mammoths. The permafrost formed and preserved their remains. The climate of Siberia and Alaska has remained cold to this day.

The geological and fossil evidence shows that the climate was much different in the past. By relying on present processes as the key to the past, the evolutionary-uniformitarian model is inadequate to explain these climate mysteries. However, the creation-Genesis flood model can easily explain these observations. Solving these many mysteries marvelously points to the fact that there was a mighty global flood as described in the Bible. Not only that, the flood resulted in a unique climate and Ice Age right after the flood.

Yosemite valley was shaped by an Ice Age glacier.

Chapter 10
Future Climate

When scientists who believe in the evolution-uniformitarian model study past climates, they conclude the earth has experienced many climate changes. They believe there were extra warm periods, and there were ice ages. One of the principles of their model is the belief that the past is the key to the future. They believe that at the present time we are living in a warm period between ice ages. Therefore, the next ice age is due soon. According to the creation-Genesis flood model, there was only one Ice Age. It was caused by the flood. Since God promised to never send a global flood again, there also will be no ice age in the future.

Before this ice age comes, these scientists also think the burning of fossil fuels will cause the greenhouse effect to grow stronger. More carbon dioxide will be added to the atmosphere. This will bring global warming and droughts in the future. The warming will melt part of the Greenland and Antarctic ice sheets causing coastal areas to flood. But is there any basis for a future greenhouse warming?

Greenhouse Warming

Carbon dioxide is one of the greenhouse gases that helps keep the earth's atmosphere warm. By studying computer experiments, scientists estimate that a doubling of carbon dioxide would cause earth's average temperature to increase about 6°F (3°C). Experience with El Niño has shown that even small temperature changes can cause dramatic shifts in weather patterns.

Since the 1950s, scientists have measured the amount of carbon dioxide in the air. They have found that is has been steadily rising. Several sources contribute to this condition. Gasoline and oil are fossil fuels, and when burned they add carbon dioxide into the atmosphere. When rain forests in the tropics are cut down, much of the carbon from the wood and the soil eventually ends up in the atmosphere. It combines with oxygen to make carbon dioxide.

From this information flowed a series of conclusions about how increased carbon dioxide would affect our world. The prospect of several degrees warming fuelled fears that long droughts may occur where most of the world's food is grown. This would result in starvation and wars. A warmer atmosphere would warm the oceans causing more frequent and much stronger hurricanes. The extra heat could melt part of the Greenland and Antarctic Ice Sheets. The meltwater would result in a higher sea level. Low areas of coastal cities would be flooded. Low wetlands, like the Florida Everglades, would be destroyed and some species would become extinct. Even the West Antarctic Ice Sheet, grounded well below sea level, might slip into the ocean. Some scientists think that a little warming could start it moving. If the ice sheet slipped into the deep ocean, sea level around the world would rise rapidly 18 feet (6 m). These are frightening warnings for the future climate.

Based on what could happen with a greenhouse warming, some scientists tell people that we must act now to prevent these tragedies. Some people say we must spent trillions of dollars to stop the warming. The rich countries must aid the poor countries. We must all live simpler lives.

Before we act, we need to first gather the facts. There is much information on the greenhouse warming that is wrong or greatly exaggerated. A video[1] on greenhouse warming even predicts an outlandish rise in world temperature of about 55°F (30°C) by the year 2050! Some environmentalists have claimed that huge amounts of tropical forests have been clear cut, especially in Brazil. However, satellite pictures have shown that these estimates for Brazil are four times too high.

There are many scientists who question much of the ominous information on greenhouse warming. One of these scientists is Dr. Robert Balling, a professor at Arizona State University. He has compiled the available data into a book named, *The Heated Debate*.[2]

The only fact that we know for sure is that carbon dioxide has increased since the 1950s. Scientists say that this increase actually has been going on since about 1850. Temperature records that go back to about 1850 show an increase of 1°F (0.6°C). However, these temperature records are in error on the warm side. One of the many errors is a result of the "heat island" effect. As cities grow, more sunshine is absorbed by houses, buildings, and concrete. The absorbed sunshine warms the atmosphere. Because of the heat island effect, Phoenix, Arizona, has warmed over 6°F (3°C). Long temperature records in or near growing cities would show warming that did not occur in the surrounding countryside.

The computer experiments that have predicted very warm temperatures for an increase in carbon dioxide are flawed. Many processes in the atmosphere are too complex to put accurately into a computer. One of these is cloud processes. Taking into consideration all these errors, Dr. Robert Balling concludes that since about 1850 the world temperature has warmed much less than 1°F (0.6°C). Therefore, he believes the greenhouse warming is true, but small.

Dr. Robert Balling also believes that a slight greenhouse warming will have little effect on the climates of the world. There is little evidence for the drought scare. The Greenland and Antarctica Ice Sheets probably would grow, not shrink or slide into the sea. This is because warmer air holds more water vapor. Therefore, sea level would not rise, but might even fall a little.

Would you make decisions that impact the world when scientists cannot agree on the amount of a global warming? They cannot even be sure whether warming will have a good or bad influence upon our environment. It is important to study the data long and carefully before we make changes in our world that would greatly change our political and economic system.

Is the Ozone Layer Decreasing?

Ozone is formed in the stratosphere when sunlight strikes oxygen. This ozone layer protects the earth from harmful ultraviolet rays. Without the ozone layer, we would all die. The little bit of ultraviolet light that does make it through the atmosphere kills excess bacteria and produces vitamin D in our skin. The ozone layer is another one of God's provisions for the protection of life on earth.

Many scientists fear that the ozone layer is decreasing due to chlorine compounds and other chemicals humans are putting into the air. Chlorofluorocarbons from spray cans, air conditioners, and refrigerators are blamed. These chemicals break down very slowly so they can be spread with time into the stratosphere. Scientists have found and measured these chemicals high in the atmosphere.

It is well-known that if the ozone layer decreases, more ultraviolet light will reach the earth's surface. If this happened there would be more cases of skin cancer and cataracts. Some scientists guess that increased ultraviolet light would also harm plants and animals, including the plankton in the sea.

In 1985 scientists discovered what is called an ozone hole around the South Pole. During the winter and early spring, ozone decreases around the South Pole. The ozone does not disappear; it just thins out for a short time.

Scientists have been trying to estimate how much the ozone around the world has decreased in the past and will decrease in the future. Although their estimates vary, they agree that the ozone layer has already decreased by a few percent. Their guesses for the future have ranged from a 3 percent to an 18 percent decrease by the year 2050. Scientists have also spent much time measuring the amount of ultraviolet light that has slipped through the ozone layer. These measure-

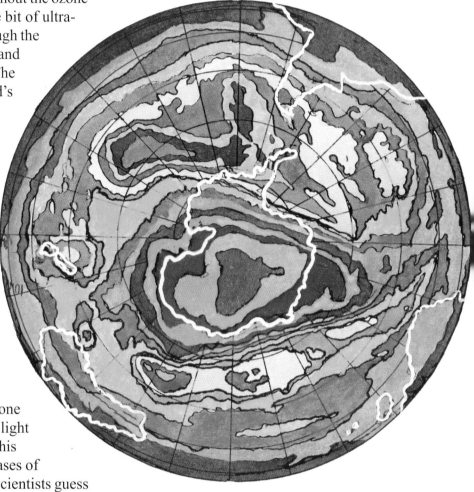

The ozone in the stratosphere over Antarctica thins out in spring, September, and October in the Southern Hemisphere. The amount of ozone is shown by different colors. The least amount of ozone is shown as the two purple areas.

ments have been chaotic. In the Swiss Alps between 1980 and 1989, scientists measured about a 6 percent increase in this radiation. Some have said there has been no change in cities because of pollution and haze absorbing the harmful rays.

In trying to figure out the cause of the ozone hole, scientists have discovered that nature is very complex. Many variables (facts that can make a difference) affect the thickness of the ozone layer. They found that the amount of ozone in the stratosphere goes in cycles. One cycle is a 2-year cycle. It is caused by the switching of the stratospheric winds over the equator. Another cycle is an 11-year sunspot cycle.

Another variable is how the air circulates in the stratosphere. This movement sometimes mixes air from the mid latitudes into the polar latitudes. The air in mid latitudes has more ozone, so when the winds carry the mid latitude air to near the pole, ozone is added. This causes the amount of ozone around the poles to vary a lot.

Scientists have also discovered that the chemical reaction between chlorofluorocarbons, the air, and other chemicals is very complicated. Some reactions increase ozone and some decrease it. The chemicals believed to destroy ozone often do not react at all.

But these chemicals will react when the stratosphere is cooler than normal. A special cloud forms, which is a combination of ice and frozen nitric acid. Only near the poles are the temperatures in the stratosphere cold enough to form this type of cloud in the winter. That is the main reason why we have an ozone "hole" near the South Pole in winter and early spring.

Volcanic dust and gases affect ozone. The volcanoes add chlorine to the stratosphere. It is now believed by many scientists that volcanoes cause much of the decrease in the ozone layer.

We still have a problem with decreased ozone due to chlorofluorocarbons in the air. Because of the other variables, the amount of ozone loss is uncertain. Just like with the greenhouse warming due to carbon dioxide, we need more information. Meanwhile, more countries are either decreasing or banning the use of chlorofluorocarbons, costing huge amounts of money.

Ozone and the Origin of Life

Ozone also presents a serious problem for those scientists who believe life evolved billions of years ago from chemicals in the ocean. They call this ocean full of chemicals the "soupy sea." They believe the earth's atmosphere had no oxygen. Life could not evolve from chemicals with oxygen in the atmosphere. But, with no oxygen, there would be no protective layer of ozone. Ozone is made from oxygen. With no ozone, ultraviolet light would bombard the surface of the earth, penetrating about 100 feet (30 m) into the soupy sea. The ultraviolet light would kill any developing life. Of course all of this assumes there really was a soupy sea and that life can develop spontaneously.

Dawn breaks over an Antarctic research station.

So, the evolutionary-uniformitarian model advocates have a problem with their theory. They cannot evolve life with oxygen in the atmosphere and they cannot do it without oxygen. Why not then conclude life had to have been created by God? This is a good question for them. The lack of ozone is just one of the many problems with the idea that life evolved from chemicals in a soupy sea.

Chapter 11
Observing the Weather

Weathermen, who are called meteorologists, measure the weather. These measurements are called observations. Observations are taken once each hour, except more often if the weather is bad. Meteorologists need weather observations to make forecasts for the weather tomorrow or in five days.

Meteorologists have sophisticated equipment to help them do their jobs. They compare readings with other weather stations nearby and around the world. Not only can they tell you what the weather is like where they are, but what is happening worldwide.

You can build your own weather station and make observations about the area where you live. It is important that you take measurements at the same time every day, and at least once a day. Keep careful records in a journal of the date and all measurements.

Weather Vane

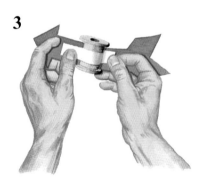

1

Cut a piece of cardboard about 8 in. (20 cm) square and mark with the points of the compass: N, S, E, and W.

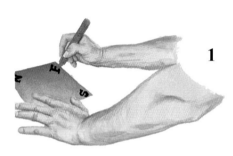

2

Tape a small piece of paper over the hole in the top of a thread spool.

3

On a piece of cardboard draw two arrows about 7 in. (18 cm) long and cut out. Tape one of the arrows to the spool.

4

Staple the second arrow to the first one. Insert a wooden dowel into modeling clay on the cardboard square. Place the spool on the dowel.

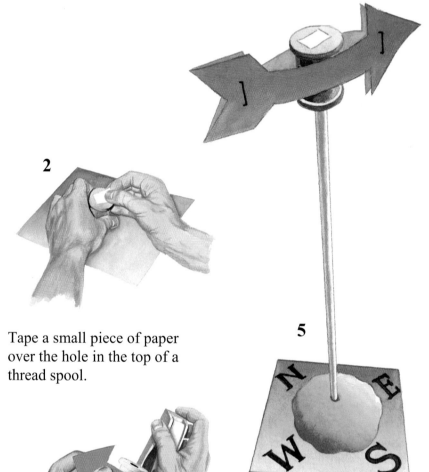

5

Using a compass, position the corners so each is pointed in the right direction. Weigh the cardboard base down so the wind won't blow it over.

Thermometers

Hang thermometers in the shade where there is good air circulation.

To make a humidity observation you need to make a wet bulb thermometer. Attach a small container to the base of a thermometer and half fill with distilled water. Wind a strip of cheesecloth around the bulb of the thermometer with the other end of the cheesecloth in the water. Compare the difference in temperature with a dry (regular) bulb thermometer and work out the relative humidity using the table below.

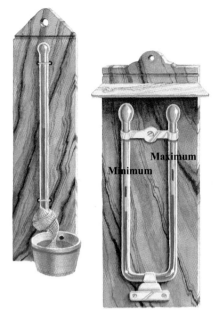

This U-shaped thermometer measures the maximum and minimum temperature range. Record the day's high, night's low, and reset for the next day.

In the National Weather Service, temperature measurements are now taken electronically.

Temperature on the dry thermometer (chart only covers 50-77°F)	Difference between wet and dry bulb thermometers										
	2°	3°	5°	7°	9°	11°	13°	14°	16°	18°	F
	1°	2°	3°	4°	5°	6°	7°	8°	9°	10°	C
50-58°F (10-14°C)	85	75	60	50	40	30	15	5	0	0	Percent Humidity
59-67°F (15-19°C)	90	80	65	60	50	40	30	20	10	5	
68-77°F (20-25°C)	90	80	70	65	55	45	40	30	25	20	

Cloud Photography

Cloud Photography is a good way to keep records of weather conditions. When you take photographs, keep a record of the date and time the picture was taken. Write the information also on the picture when it is developed. Add the cloud type if you know it.

Abbreviations for cloud types:

Altocumulus - Ac   Cumulonimbus - Cb
Altostratus - As   Cumulus - Cu
Cirrocumulus - Cc   Nimbostratus - Ns
Cirrostratus - Cs   Stratocumulus - Sc
Cirrus - Ci   Stratus - St

Condensation Experiment

This expirement shows how condensation forms as warm air is cooled. First, pour very hot water (not boiling, as the jar might break) into a glass jar.

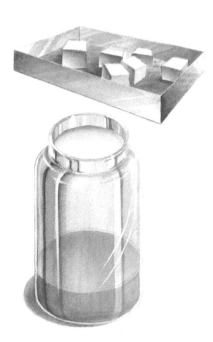

Next, place ice cubes on a metal tray or plate. Place on top of the jar.

As the air is cooled by the ice cubes, water vapor condenses on the sides of the jar.

Barometer

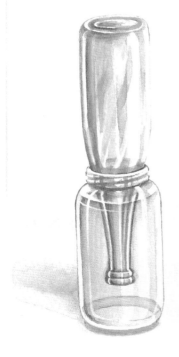  

Set a bottle upside-down in a jar. The top of the bottle should not touch the bottom of the jar.

Pour enough colored water in the jar so that the top of the bottle is just covered.

Mark the water level on the jar. Make several other marks for comparisons (or tape a ruler to side of jar). Place where the temperature is fairly constant. Record changes over the next several weeks.

Barometers are used by weathermen to measure the weight of the air, or air pressure. When the barometer measures a "low" pressure, the weather is often stormy. "High" pressure brings mostly clear weather. The air does not feel heavier or lighter to you because the difference is very small; but it makes a *big* difference to the weather. To make accurate observations, you might consider purchasing a barometer at a store.

Weather Balloons

Weather Balloons — Weather does not occur just at the ground. The weatherman needs to take measurements in the atmosphere also. To learn what the weather is like high in the atmosphere, the weatherman sends up weather balloons. These balloons have weather instruments and a radio transmitter tied to them. The radio transmits information about the temperature, pressure, and amount of water vapor. A radar back at the weather station tracks the balloon to learn the wind speed and direction in the atmosphere. Weather balloons are sent up twice a day at the same time all over the world. The six-foot-wide (2 m) balloon is filled with hydrogen gas. It usually rises to about 100,000 feet (30,480 m). As the balloon rises, it grows to be as big as a house. It pops and a parachute gently lowers it to the ground so no one is injured. If you find one of these weather balloons, you can return the instrument to the weather station and keep the balloon.

Rain Gauge

Precipitation is measured in a rain gauge. One inch of rainfall means that rain, one inch deep, fell over the area. Of course, if you stick a ruler in a mud puddle there is more water there. That is because water ran from the surrounding area and collected in the puddle. The rain gauge measures only the rain that fell in the bottle and not water that flowed into it.

If it is snowing, some rain gauges automatically melt the snow. Otherwise, the weather observer must melt it. The measurement of precipitation is mostly automatic. Measuring snow depth is still done by going outside and sticking a ruler in the snow that is not disturbed by wind or other factors.

Using a sharp pair of scissors, cut the top off a clear plastic bottle that has a flat bottom. Make the cut 4 to 6 in. (10 to 15 cm) from the top. Turn the top of the bottle over and tape to bottom.

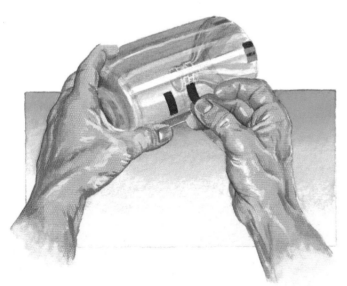

Adhere thin strips of 1 in. (2.5 cm) tape to the side of the bottle (or tape a ruler). Start the tape (or zero point of the ruler) 1 inch up from the bottom. When assembled fill the bottle with water up to the 1-inch mark.

Set your gauge in a bucket to stabilize and protect it. Make sure the rim of the bucket doesn't come much over the edge of your gauge. Set out away from buildings or trees.

Chapter 12
God, Creation, and You

God is the Creator (Colossians 1:16). He has placed us in charge of His wonderful creation. Genesis 1:28 says that people are to "be fruitful and increase in number; fill the earth and subdue it. Rule over the fish of the sea and the birds of the air and over every living creature that moves on the ground." Indeed, we are in charge and we do rule over all the animals and the plants. However, some people misinterpret this verse and claim it gives people permission to harm the environment and destroy the earth. They blame Christians for many of our environmental problems and for possibly changing the future climate. This verse does not mean that we are to destroy God's wonderful creation. You can go back to Genesis and read verse 2:15 which says: "The Lord God took man and put him in the Garden of Eden to work it and take care of it." Although we are in charge of God's creation, we have been given the responsibility to *take care* of it.

Therefore, we should be concerned about greenhouse warming, the ozone layer, and air

pollution. We should not be polluting the earth ourselves, and we should support those who are trying to fix environmental problems. However, we must have a reasonably clear idea of what the problem is before we can fix it. Too many people have wanted to spend billions of dollars to stop greenhouse warming. They have urged us to act before we have understood the problem. Further research on greenhouse warming shows there is a problem, but it is not as serious as the doomsayers proclaim. The decrease of the ozone layer is a more serious problem and has better scientific support.

Some of the people who urge action to save the environment may have other reasons besides concern for the environment. Some urge that we live simpler lives. A few claim we need to go "back to nature." They say we will stop polluting the planet if we drastically change our lifestyle. However, very poor countries, where the people live so-called

in environmental issues. Their motivation is love for God's creation and concern for His people and animals. As Christians, we should be able to join together with non-Christians to solve legitimate environmental issues.

The Christian realizes the most serious pollution problem is sin. It is man who does evil, including polluting the environment. Unless we deal with the evil in man's heart by bringing people to Jesus, there is little hope for progress toward a better environment. The Christian should be involved in eliminating both kinds of pollution.

simple lives, have severe environmental problems. The "simple lives" of the Indians in Brazil cause them to cut down and burn their rain forests. The countries that lived under socialism in the former Soviet Union also have severe environmental problems. So living "simple lives" will not necessarily bring about a better environment. In fact, the environment of technologically advanced North America has some of the cleanest air, water, and streets of any area in the world.

A few environmentalists, called pantheists, believe animals, trees, the environment, and the earth are god. If everything is god, why should we even be concerned about pollution and the environment? If the earth were god, it could take care of itself. Pantheism seems to be anti-environmental.

Many environmentalists try to convince us that man is a risen animal. They believe we have no more right to the earth than other animals. Their basic assumption is the theory of evolution. However, animals have no concern for their environment. How can the belief that we are risen animals really help the environmental problem? They do not understand that mankind is made in God's image and likeness. The creation was made by God. Therefore, we should respect and take care of God's creation.

Most environmentalists are genuinely concerned for the environment. Some are committed Christians who have been led to become involved

Index

Illustration/Photo Credits

t-top, b-bottom, c-center, l-left, r-right

Lloyd R. Hight (illustrations): 10-11, 15, 17-22, 24, 26-31, 33, 36, 38-40, 43-44, 46, 49-51, 54, 56, 63, 67-68, 70, 717, 72, 74-77
Earl and Bonita Snellenberger (illustrations): 7t, 65, 66
Corel Stock Photography Library: 2-5, 10, 12-13, 21, 23, 24b, 25cl cr bl, 31b, 54, 57-61, 64, 69b, 71, 73, 78-79, 80
Byron Aughenbaugh (photography): 24t, 25tl tr br, 26, 29, 31t, 32-34, 35b, 36-39, 62
National Oceanic and Atmospheric Administration: 44, 45br, 47tr, 49-50, 52-53, 56
National Center for Atmospheric Research: 41t
Expert Photo CD Gallery #2: 48
U.S. Geological Survey Photographic Library: 69t
Jim Campbell: 46b
Charles Doswell III: 42t   Steve Keighton: 46
Ted Fathauer: 55   Doug Laubach: 41b
Joseph Golden: 47tr   Mike Oard: 45t, 47l

Endnotes

[1] *The Fragile Planet: Alterations in the Atmosphere* (Princeton, NJ: Films for the Humanities and Sciences, 1990).
[2] Robert C. Balling, *The Heated Debate: Greenhouse Predictions Versus Climate Reality* (San Francisco, CA: Pacific Research Institute for Public Policy, 1992).

Thunderheads (cumulonimbus) building over California coast near San Francisco.

Glossary

arid — a dry climate lacking moisture.

atmosphere — the body of gasses surrounding the earth.

axis — an imaginary straight line through the center of the earth on which it rotates.

ball lightning — a glowing ball of red, orange, or yellow light found during a thunderstorm.

barometer — a weather instrument used to measure the pressure of the atmosphere.

blizzard — a very heavy snowstorm with violent winds.

bogs — soft, waterlogged ground such as a marsh.

carbon dioxide — a colorless, odorless gas formed during respiration, combustion, and organic decomposition.

chinook winds — foehn winds that are mild, gusty, west winds found along the east slopes of the Rocky Mountains.

cirrus clouds — a high altitude cloud made of ice crystals that appear thin, white, and feathery.

climate — the weather conditions that are particular to a certain area, such as wind, precipitation, and temperature.

cold front — a boundary of cold air, usually moving from the north or west, which is displacing the warm air.

condensation — the act of water vapor changing from a gas to a liquid.

convection clouds — clouds that occur in a rising updraft, usually when the sun's radiation warms the earth. This causes the water vapor to condense.

Coriolis force — the movement of atmospheric air caused by the rotating earth.

cumulus clouds — low clouds that are thick, white, and puffy with flat bottoms and rounded tops.

dew point — the temperature at which air becomes saturated and dew forms.

Doppler radar — a special type of radar used to track severe weather by detecting wind speed and direction.

downdraft — a downward current of air.

electricity — a moving electric charge, such as in a thunderstorm.

electrons — a subatomic particle with a negative electrical charge.

El Niño — a warm current from the west that replaces the cool ocean current along Peru and Ecuador.

environment — the surrounding circumstances or conditions around us.

equator — an imaginary line dividing the northern and southern hemispheres of the earth.

evaporation — to change into a vapor such as the evaporation of water by the warming of the sun.

flash flood — a flood caused by a thunderstorm that deposits an unusual amount of rain on a particular area.

fog — clouds that form on the surface of the ground.

fossil fuels — coal and oil derived from the remains of plant and animal organisms.

greenhouse warming — the phenomena of a steady, gradual rise of temperatures due to the increase of carbon dioxide in the atmosphere. This could result in natural catastrophes such as droughts, flooding, and a meltdown of the ice sheets.

hailstones — precipitation in the form of ice and hard snow pellets.

humid — a weather condition containing a large amount of moisture or water vapor.

hurricane — the strongest storm found in the tropics, with heavy rain and winds of 75 mph or greater.

Ice Age — a period of time marked by extensive glaciers on the face of the earth.

ice cap — an extensive covering of ice and snow.

ice storm — a storm caused by rain falling into a lower atmosphere that is below freezing.

Intertropical Convergence Zone — area near the equator where winds from different directions merge or mix.

latitudes — the distance north or south of the equator measured with imaginary lines on a map or globe.

meteorologist — a person that interprets scientific data and forecasts the weather for a specific area.

monsoon — a wind system that causes periods of wet and dry weather in India and southern Asia.

nitrogen — a naturally occurring element that is responsible for around four-fifths of the earth's atmosphere.

Northeaster — a storm that moves northeast along the east coast.

oxygen — a colorless, odorless gas that is 21 percent of our atmosphere. It is essential for plant and animal respiration.

ozone — a gas in the earth's upper atmosphere that is responsible for screening most of the sun's harmful ultraviolet radiation.

permafrost — permanently frozen subsoil found around polar regions.

plankton — tiny plant and animal organisms found in the oceans.

pollution —harmful or unsafe waste products.

precipitation — falling moisture in the form of rain, sleet, snow, hail, or drizzle.

rain gauge — a weather instrument used to measure the amount of rainfall over a particular period of time.

relative humidity — the amount of water vapor in the air compared to the amount of water vapor the air can contain at the point of saturation.

Santa Ana winds — a foehn wind that blows westward from the mountains of southern California to the coast when a high pressure area settles over Nevada, Utah, and Idaho.

sleet — precipitation that consists of frozen raindrops.

static electricity — a build-up of electrical charge on an insulated body.

St. Elmo's fire — a condition caused by a high charge of electricity in the air that causes pointed objects to glow slightly.

stratus clouds — low altitude gray clouds with a flat base.

subarctic — a region just south of the Arctic Circle.

supercell — a severe, well-organized thunderstorm with warm moist air spiraling upwards.

thermometer — an instrument used to indicate the temperature.

thunderstorm — a condition of weather that produces thunder, lightning, and rain.

tide — a raising and lowering of the water in the oceans and seas caused by the gravitational pull of the moon. The sun causes some, but to a lesser degree.

tornado — a funnel-shaped column of air rotating up to 300 mph, touching the ground.

tropical — a warm climate located near the equator, usually having lots of precipitation.

tropical depression — rainstorms with winds of 38 mph or less.

tropical storm — a storm of heavy rain and winds between 39 and 74 mph.

tundra — a region usually located at high altitude. The ground is permanently frozen.

typhoon — another name for a hurricane.

ultraviolet light — the range of wavelengths just beyond violet in the visible spectrum. Invisible to humans, yet capable of causing skin cancer.

updraft — an upward current of air.

warm front — a boundary of warm air which is pushing out cold air in the atmosphere.

water vapor — invisible water distributed throughout the atmosphere.

weather balloons — balloons used to carry weather instruments into the atmosphere to gather data.

weather vane — an instrument used to indicate wind direction.

wind chill factor — the temperature of windless air that would have the same cooling effect on exposed skin as a combination of wind speed and air temperature.